DIVE
Devotions

Bryan Keeley

FAITH
ALIVE®
Christian Resources

Grand Rapids, Michigan

Dive Devotions, 2011 Faith Alive Christian Resources, Grand Rapids, Michigan.

Printed in the United States of America.

Any questions or comments on this book? We'd love to hear from you: editors@faithaliveresources.org.

Illustrations by April Hartman

ISBN 978-1-59255-677-9

10 9 8 7 6 5 4 3 2 1

About This Book

Hi!

I wrote this book for YOU. OK, maybe not you personally, but I hope you like it anyway. Here's what you'll find inside:

- Interactive readings—three per week. Sounds doable, right?
- Story symbols. They look like this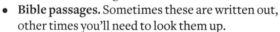

If you're using this book along with Dive for Sunday school or youth group, the symbols will match the stories you explore together at church. Look for a new symbol at the beginning of each week's readings.

- **Bible passages.** Sometimes these are written out, other times you'll need to look them up.
- **Q&As.** These are short summaries of the teachings of the Reformed/Presbyterian church. We'll look at one or two each week.
- **Questions.** Each reflection comes with a question. Ponder it yourself or talk it over with a friend, parent, or mentor.
- **Challenges.** These help you dive in a little deeper. Who doesn't like a good challenge?
- **Christmas and Easter readings.** These are meant for the week of Christmas and Easter. Find them when the time comes; skip them if you reach them too soon.
- **Sketches and doodles.** These are just for fun. Add your own to make it personal.

When you read this book you'll need to have a Bible nearby and a pencil or pen in hand—you never know when you might be asked to sketch a UFO, draw a timeline of your life, or name three of your best friends.

Talk to God about your thoughts and reactions to each reading. Most of all, use this book to help you grow in faith, connect with God's people, and live out God's story for your life.

Bryan

A Few More Things . . .

How is this book organized?

Dive Devotions is part of a curriculum called *Dive* that many churches use for Sunday school or youth group. For each Dive session there are three readings that build on what happened in church that week. These may be about the story, the Q&A, or the Memory Challenge. With each reading you'll have the chance to dive in a little deeper.

What if my church isn't using the Dive curriculum?

No worries, you can use this book on its own. Just go at your own pace and enjoy the stories, Q&A's, and the time you spend with God.

Where do the Q&A's come from?

The Q&A's used in this book are a short summary of creeds and confessions of the Reformed/Presbyterian tradition called *Q&A: A Summary of Biblical Teachings.* They include teachings from the Heidelberg Catechism, Belgic Confession, and the Canons of Dort.

Why do the Christmas and Easter readings come at the end of the book?

These readings are at the end of the book so that you can easily find them when Christmas and Easter arrive. If you're using this book as part of the Dive curriculum, you'll celebrate Easter and Christmas with a session at church and then read the three devotions during the following week. If you're using this book on your own, read them leading up to or following these special days of the church year.

Belonging

What is your only comfort as a Christian?
That I, body and soul, in life and death,
belong to Jesus Christ.

—Q&A 1

On Facebook I belong to lots of different groups. One group I belong to is Camp Greenwood. It's one of my favorites because I can reconnect with friends from years ago, see pictures of what is going on at camp, and share stories with other campers.

But I also have things that belong to me, like my bike, my iPod, and my cell phone. These two ways of belonging mean very different things. The first "belong" means being a member, like the way a puzzle piece belongs to a puzzle. The puzzle doesn't own it, but the piece belongs to the puzzle. The second "belong" is possessive; like the puzzles that I have at home—they belong to me, I own them.

So what is my only comfort in life and in death? That I belong, like a puzzle piece. I was made to be here! I'm a member of a community, the church. I'm a unique part of God's family because I belong to Jesus. My life fits into God's big-picture plan for the whole world!

Can you name

A deacon at your church: _____

An elder: _____

3 Adults (not related to you): _____

2 Kids: _____

2 Teenagers: _____

1 Friend _____

WELCOME TO "NAME THAT DEACON!"

THINK ABOUT IT   TALK ABOUT IT

Do you **feel** like you belong in your church? Why or Why not?

What could you do to help someone else feel like they belong this week?

The End of the Story

Read Acts 16:16-25.

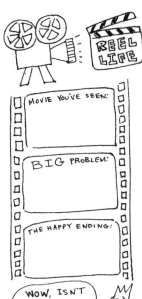

Wait, what? You're going to stop the story there? Paul and Silas get thrown into prison and beaten, their feet in stocks. What about the good part? When do we get to read the part about the earthquake and the prison doors flying open? It's like watching the first half of *Return of the Jedi* without getting to see the Ewok battle scene!

NO WAY, IT'S LIKE WATCHING _____

WITHOUT _____

Think about the movies you have seen recently. Have you noticed there is usually a problem that makes the main character uncomfortable? But no fear, you know that within 120 minutes that problem will be fixed somehow. Nearly every movie is a story of problems that are quickly fixed. But in life it's not that easy. Some problems we live with for a long, long time.

In real life, there are people who make you think you're worthless. They tell you you're not good enough. There are problems that you don't know how to fix. Life isn't full of quick, easy solutions—but we know the end of the story! No matter what happens, no matter what problems we face, "whether we live or die, we belong to the Lord" (Romans 14:8). That's a promise!

THINK ABOUT IT TALK ABOUT IT

Here's what's happening lately . . .

CHALLENGE

Take some time to talk to God about a not-so-easy-to-fix problem. It could be yours or someone else's.

MY NEW MOTTO!

Then repeat after me (out loud) "Whatever happens, I still belong to Jesus."

6

Comfort

What is your only comfort as a Christian?
That I, body and soul, in life and in death, belong to Jesus Christ.
—*Q&A 1*

We all know the feeling—when summer vacation starts, when that long piano recital finally ends, when the dentist says, "No cavities!" It's a feeling of freedom: release from teachers, flat notes, and dentists. It's the feeling we know every night when we curl up in our warm bed—*comfort*.

The world has thousands of ways to make us comfortable. From air conditioning to Snuggies, massage chairs to ergonomic headphones, travel mugs to tag-free shirts. But in today's Q&A we're asked "What is your *only* comfort in life and in death?" You mean I have to pick just one?

Paul and Silas, in Acts 16:16-25, were beaten and thrown into prison with their feet tied up because they sent an evil spirit out of a girl who was enslaved. They weren't comfortable at all. But what did they do? They sang hymns to God.

I'M MOST COMFORTABLE WHEN: _____

It's easy to focus on how comfortable we feel right now. But the comfort and relief we feel after completing tests and homework, or facing a piano recital or dentist appointment, only lasts for a short time. The comfort of knowing that we belong to Jesus Christ lasts for an eternity. It can even make going to the dentist seem like not such a big deal anymore!

MY COMFORTABLE CLOTHES

SALE

100% WORRY FREE

I NEED COMFORT WHEN: _____

CHALLENGE

Think of a Christian song or hymn that you like. Or maybe a favorite verse. Make it the soundtrack to your day. When you start getting stressed out, turn on that song in your mind and see what happens.

THINK ABOUT IT   TALK ABOUT IT

My biggest stressors:

How can I turn my ~~bad~~ thoughts to God when I'm STRESSED OUT?!

How Can *I* Belong?

What must you know to have this comfort?

First, how I sin every day against God and my neighbor; second, how Jesus saves me from my sin; third, how I can show my thanks by gladly serving God in everything I do.

—Q&A 2

MY FAVORITE INFOMERCIAL

ACT NOW AND WE'LL DOUBLE YOUR ORDER!

Have you ever seen one of those infomercials you can quote after seeing it just a few times? You know the ones: the new cleaning device, electronic gadget, or exercise equipment that will make your life so much better. They usually end like this: "Just three easy payments of $19.95." What an amazing offer!

Sometimes the salesperson will ask the audience, "Would you like to know how you can get one of these (insert magical gadget here)?" This sales question is kind of like Q&A 2. In Q&A 1 we learn what God has to offer us (deep comfort through belonging). In Q&A 2 we find out how we can get it.

1. WE SIN

The list is simple; we must know three things: that we sin every day against God and other people; that Jesus saves us from our sin; and that we can show our thanks by gladly serving God in everything we do. These are the three things we'll be looking at together. The good news is that there are no payments—not even easy ones. Jesus already paid for us. Now *that's* an amazing offer!

THINK ABOUT IT   TALK ABOUT IT

Have you trusted Jesus to save you from your sin?

2. JESUS SAVES US

3. WE SERVE GOD!

CHALLENGE

Name four ways you can show your thanks by serving God this week:

1 _____
2 _____
3 _____
4 _____

For Sure!

Read Acts 16:25-40.

How does faith work in your life?

There I was, about to climb to the top of a 40-foot telephone pole and jump off it to ring a bell. I would be dangling four stories above the ground with nothing but a small harness and rope to hold me. I have to tell you—I was a little nervous.

I turned to the high ropes instructor and asked what I thought was a reasonable question. "Are you sure this will hold me?" I didn't want to fall to my death. As he strapped me in he explained that last week a 300-pound man had made the same jump with the equipment I was wearing and was safely and slowly returned to the ground. Considering I weigh 160 pounds, I found that statement pretty comforting.

I wonder if the jailer in Acts 16 was in a similar situation. He wasn't sure about what was going to happen either. He thought he might also lose his life because the prisoners had escaped. He wasn't sure what he needed to do to be saved, and he was nervous.

What if the jailer had asked Paul and Silas, "Are you sure we will be saved if we believe?" I wonder if Paul and Silas would have explained that the week before, a woman in Philippi (Acts 16:11-15) had believed and was saved. "The same grace that saves her can save you too!" they might have said.

I needed that harness and rope to catch me after the jump. And before I would jump, I needed to be sure it would catch me. In the same way that the high ropes instructor assured me, Paul assured the jailer: "Believe in the Lord Jesus, and you will be saved." That assurance is for you too!

You probably aren't worried about prisoners escaping or about falling from a telephone pole—at least I hope you're not. But you might be worried about whether faith really works. It worked for Paul and Silas. It worked for the jailer. It works for me. And it will work for you too.

CHALLENGE

This week, ask a Christian (a friend or parent or someone else) if he or she is sure that we will be saved if we believe in Jesus. Find out what makes the person sure or unsure.

9

THINK ABOUT IT   TALK ABOUT IT

When you are going through a hard time, how do you lean on Jesus?

Earthquake!

Believe in the Lord Jesus, and you will be saved—you and your household.

—Acts 16:31

When I was in the eighth grade, there was a big thunderstorm in Holland, Michigan, my hometown. My parents took my sisters and me down to the basement to seek shelter. We listened to the wind blow and thunder rumble and then it happened: a huge old tree in our backyard fell with a giant CRACK!

Hearing the noise, we trembled in fear, wondering what damage had been done. My dad went upstairs to find that the tree had fallen perfectly between our house and our back fence, filling our yard with branches and leaves but leaving the house unharmed. Though our house had lost power, we all breathed a big sigh of relief.

This storm hit too close to home . . .

If you've been part of a natural disaster like a thunderstorm, a tornado, or an earthquake, you know it can be very scary—much worse than I've described. I bet the jailer in Acts 16 felt the same way. On top of the fear of the earthquake was the fear that he was going to lose his job. Imagine his relief when he found out that despite the earthquake and jailbreak, everything was going to be OK.

Because of sin, our world is broken. People are starving to death. Greed and lust are part of our lives; pollution, disease, and war fill our newspapers. But just like the relief my family felt when we saw that the tree had missed our house, we can breathe a sigh of relief when we realize that even disasters can't separate us from the love of Christ.

How does Jesus bring hope, even in these situations?

CHALLENGE

List three ways you see that the world is broken.

1 _____
2 _____
3 _____

The Greatest

Jesus replied, "Love the Lord your God with all your heart and with all your soul and with all your mind." This is the first and greatest commandment. And the second is like it: "Love your neighbor as yourself."

—Matthew 22:37-40

GOD

FOR ME, LOVING GOD MEANS:

My dad and I both play guitar. He's been doing it a *lot* longer than I have, so he's managed to accumulate some pretty nice guitars over the years. Sometimes I borrow one, but I don't always borrow the same one. It's hard to say which one's my favorite. There's the one I learned on (an old Telecaster), so that one is important to me. But his other guitars are pretty cool too. I'd have a hard time saying that one is "better" that the other ones.

One day one of the experts of the law asked Jesus what the "greatest commandment" was. That was a tough question, too. It was also a trick question. It wasn't like they were asking Jesus to pick a best friend or a favorite guitar. They figured that if he picked one of the commandments they could criticize him for not picking one of the others.

Jesus' answer surprised them: he picked the *Shema*, a section of Deuteronomy 6 that starts with "Hear O Israel, the Lord our God, the Lord is one" and then goes on to say, "Love the Lord your God with all your heart and with all your soul and all your strength." And then Jesus surprised them again by adding another command—love your neighbor as yourself.

UGH...
THESE PEOPLE ARE REALLY HARD FOR ME TO LOVE

Basically Jesus told them that love was the answer. That sounds really easy, doesn't it? But it turns out that it's a lot harder than we think (because of the sin inside of us). Even though I am supposed to love God first and love other people, I actually spend a lot more time loving myself and putting my wants ahead of what other people need. Every once in a while I realize what I'm doing and I don't like it. It reminds me just how much I need the love of Jesus to fill me.

THINK ABOUT IT *TALK ABOUT IT*

What's harder for you, loving God or loving your neighbor?

CHALLENGE *Today!!! keep track of the times you think of yourself first . . .*

Feeling Guilty

"Love the Lord your God with all your heart and with all your soul and with all your mind." This is the first and greatest commandment. And the second is like it: "Love your neighbor as yourself."

—Matthew 22:37-40

CHALLENGE

Today, pay attention to that guilty feeling you get when you do something wrong—then stop and pray about it, right then. Know that you are forgiven.

THINK ABOUT IT **TALK ABOUT IT**

Why is sin sometimes fun even though it's wrong?

It was fall, and I was in the sixth grade. I was hiding behind big pile of leaves with a friend. We were just goofing around and started throwing sticks trying to hit cars. We figured we were hidden and could get away with it. We actually hit a couple of cars and were having a lot of fun.

Then one of the cars we hit came to a stop down the block and turned around. My friend and I were terrified. We hopped on our bikes and took off as fast as we could. After riding through a few people's lawns to get away, we knew we had to hide. So we doubled back to my parents' house to seek cover in the backyard.

It wasn't long before my mom opened the back door and yelled "BRYAN!" You know how sometimes all that your mom has to do is say your name and you know you're in trouble? I knew I was caught.

The interesting thing is, while we were throwing the sticks we were having fun. It was a great time! But when that car turned around all the fun turned to fear and I felt really guilty for what I had done. I felt guilty because I knew I had done wrong.

When we feel guilty for things we do or say, we know that we are broken and sinful. I remember how lousy I felt when that car stopped. I hated that feeling. I'm glad I don't feel that way all the time, but maybe we all should feel it a little more often. Then we wouldn't wait until we're caught to confront the sin in our lives.

I THREW STICKS AT CARS. WHAT HAVE YOU DONE THAT YOU KNOW IS WRONG?

CRACK!

SCREEEEECH!

Siblings

Read Genesis 4:1-16.

MY SISTER ACTING LIKE A CHICKEN
LOL

I have a twin sister. For as long as I can remember, we've been competitive. When we were in kindergarten we each wanted to prove that we were better than the other. One day I told her that if she walked around nodding her head like a chicken that would make her cool. So the following day at school she walked around nodding her head like a chicken. (Hey, she was only five.) When she realized that it was *not* a cool thing to do, she was very upset with me. (That's actually putting it mildly.)

Sibling rivalry has been around for a while. In fact, Cain and Abel had the first sibling rivalry in history, and things haven't changed much since then. All of us are affected by sin. Whether we realize it or not, we selfishly strive to make ourselves seem better by putting others down.

Although I never killed my sister, I've said and done things that hurt her. I'm sorry about that. But I still find myself doing it. My (sinful) nature tells me to fight for myself to prove that I am the best. But God tells me to love my neighbor as myself. I'm working on it, but I have a way to go. How about you?

TOP **5** REASONS I FIGHT WITH MY SIBLINGS (OR OTHER PEOPLE'S SIBLINGS):

1 _____
2 _____
3 _____
4 _____
5 _____

WHAT ABOUT PEOPLE WHO GET ON MY NERVES? HOW DO I LOVE THEM?

CHALLENGE

I could love my sibling—or my "neighbor"—by

1
2
3

THINK ABOUT IT   TALK ABOUT IT

Cain sarcastically asked God, "Am I my brother's keeper?" Does God expect you to be anyone else's keeper? What does that even mean?

Choose Love

If we live, we live to the Lord; and if we die, we die to the Lord. So, whether we live or die, we belong to the Lord.
—Romans 14:8

MY FAVORITE DONUT IS:

One day I was at the donut shop picking up a couple dozen donuts for our high school mission trip. The woman working there asked me what all the donuts were for and found out I worked for a church. So she asked me a question she had about God. "If God is in complete control, why did God let Adam and Eve sin?"

WHAT WOULD THE WORLD BE LIKE IF WE COULDN'T CHOOSE GOOD ?? OR EVIL?

This is a question I've also struggled with, and I shared with her one of the best explanations I've heard. I told her that if she had kids and they only had the choice to love her, their love wouldn't be as meaningful as it is when they have the choice to love or not to love.

TO LOVE OR NOT TO LOVE... THAT IS THE QUESTION

When we were created, God gave us the choice to love him or not to love him. This is what makes our relationship meaningful. Although God loves us no matter what, we have to make a choice to love God—and we also have to make a choice to love those around us.

Love is more than just a feeling, though. When we really love someone it shows in the way we *act*. And God told us how to act in his law. Unfortunately we don't do that very well. At least I know that I don't. Do you?

THINK ABOUT IT / TALK ABOUT IT

Do I really love God, or do I just say I love God because that's what I'm supposed to do?

CHALLENGE

Write a love letter to God. Or list three other ways you show God love by what you do:

☆

☆

☆

HAPPY MOTHER'S DAY...

Dear Mom,
As require
I love
you.

Jr.

XO

Totally Sinful

Why don't you do what God wants?
I naturally tend to sin, sometimes on purpose, sometimes without thinking. I am like this because the first man and woman, Adam and Eve, chose to disobey their Creator and become sinners. They did this even though they were made in God's own image, good and obedient.

—Q&A 4

Q: How sinful are you?
A: *No part of my life is free of sin.*

—Q&A 5

Though some of the teens at my church might disagree, I think I'm pretty amazing at creating puns. On St. Patrick's Day I posted this pun on my Facebook page: "Don't iron your St. Patrick's Day shirt. You don't want to press your luck." Funny, right?

Here's the thing—my dad does puns too (of course he's not as good at them as I am). It turns out that lots of things, from my habits to my looks, have been passed down to me from my parents. It's a basic fact of life— we all look or act a little like the people who raised us.

Our great-great-great-great—and so on—grandparents, Adam and Eve, passed stuff on to us too. I don't know if I have Adam's chin or if Eve ate pizza the way I do, but there is one thing that I *know* they passed down to me. Sin.

Sin isn't just something I do on occasion—it's deep down in me, in my DNA. The bad stuff I do affects every part of my life. It's like putting a drop of ink in a glass full of water. Soon the whole glass gets inky.

It would be easy for me to say I can't help making bad choices, that I'm just built that way. But at the end of the day, it's still my responsibility. I'm still choosing to put my wants and will ahead of God's. Just because I picked that up from my great-great-great grandparents doesn't mean it isn't *my* sin.

THINK ABOUT IT TALK ABOUT IT

Why is it so hard to own up to the bad things we do?

CHALLENGE What are some of the good things that have been passed down to you from your family?

AUNT CEILIA'S
SECRET SPAGHETTI SAUCE

Why Don't I Do What God Wants?

We all have it—the natural tendency to lose sight of what we're supposed to be doing. When does that happen in your life?

Have you ever had an assignment to do and you just couldn't make yourself do it? I'm that way. Even with things that I really want to do, I find myself distracted. For instance, as I'm writing this section I'm sitting at my computer. I have some music on so I take a break to check on what song I'm listening to. Then I check to see what song comes next. Then I think about a cool way to change my iTunes playlist so it automatically give me random songs I like.

I realize that I should get back to work, so I begin writing again. But then I think about my sister on her spring break choir tour. I wonder if she's making progress on her trip to the East Coast so I check Facebook for an update.... I check my phone too, to see if she's sent me a text. Wonder what route they're taking from Michigan to New York City? I should check Google maps to see how they're going to get there. I wonder what they'll be seeing in New York?

♪ OH, SAY CAN YOU SEE... ♪

Thinking about my sister is great, but I am not getting stuff done that needs to be done. Something inside of me keeps me distracted. I'm that way with other things too— and so are you. I'm not just talking about little stuff like homework. I'm talking about the really important stuff, like the way we act in everyday life.

We know what we ought to be doing, but sin keeps our attention from focusing on that stuff. Often we end up doing other things instead. In the last devotional we talked about how we're totally sinful. That doesn't mean I can't do good things, but it does mean that no part of my life is without sin. Sin shows up in my behavior and in the way that I think about things.

CHALLENGE

Pray about it, using these words or your own: God, I'm sorry for losing track of what I should be doing. I have a tendency to sin, sometimes on purpose, and sometimes without even realizing it. Thank you for forgiving all of my sins!

POP QUIZ

Q: WHAT IS THE MOST IMPORTANT THING THAT SIN DISTRACTS US FROM?

A: _____

Hint: 4 LETTER WORD THAT WE CAN CHOOSE... LOOK 2 PAGES BACK.

God Is Just

Read Genesis 6-7.

As a child I was pretty carefree. Nothing could take me down (at least that's what I thought). My parents used to tell me to think about the consequences of the things I did. I would eat snow, drink caffeinated soda right before bed, and ride my bike down the stairs. Consequences were far from my mind. Even breaking my arm snowboarding didn't slow me down much.

Now that I'm a little older I'm discovering that if I drink caffeine before bed I won't get to sleep for hours. I found out the hard way that my bike deserves a little more respect. It turns out that actions really do have consequences. Who knew?

Sin has consequences too, and the people in the flood story were sinning a lot—both without thinking and on purpose. "Every inclination of the thoughts of the human heart was only evil all the time" (Genesis 6:5). Every human heart, that is, except Noah's. "He walked faithfully with God" (Genesis 6:9). Though he was still sinful, Noah didn't *want* to sin. He wanted to have a good relationship with God.

CRAZY THINGS I DID AS A CHILD:

_____
_____
_____
_____

Noah didn't save himself—God saved him. But we can't ignore what happened to all the other people. It turns out that the consequences of our sin are a lot more serious than lost sleep or bumps and bruises. God is serious about sin. The people were bent on evil and their lives were full of sin, so God wiped them from the earth.

WHY DID I DRINK THAT THIRD MOUNTAIN DEW?

CHALLENGE

Pray about it:
God, I'm sorry for _____ I want to live your way, but I know I can only do that through the forgiveness of Jesus Christ. Amen

THINK ABOUT IT — TALK ABOUT IT

Besides me, who is affected by my sin?

TRUE STORY

Whenever I complained about things being unfair, my parents quickly reminded me that everything I had was a gift from them or someone else. They said that if I want it to be fair, they would just take it back . . .

MINE, ALL MINE

God Is Merciful

Read Genesis 8.

When I was growing up I was convinced that everything had to be fair—especially when it came to me and my twin sister. To me, "fair" meant getting exactly the same thing—or maybe a little more. If it wasn't fair, I let my parents know! From sitting shotgun in the car to computer, time I wanted to make sure I got what I deserved.

Here's the cool thing about Christianity—it teaches us that we *don't* get what we deserve. If our relationship with God was "fair" we would be in serious trouble. Because of our sin, we'd be in the same boat as those people in the flood (actually, we wouldn't have a boat at all).

Thankfully our relationship with God isn't based on fairness. We don't get what we deserve—we get something much, much better! The Bible says, "If we confess our sins, he is faithful and just and will forgive us our sins and purify us from all unrighteousness" (1 John 1:9).

Aren't you glad life isn't fair? God offers us forgiveness because he is both just and merciful. All we have to do is confess our sins and ask for forgiveness. Then we can walk with God like Noah, and we can show God love by living according to his will.

THINK ABOUT IT TALK ABOUT IT

Things that have to be fair in my family:

CHALLENGE

List some ways you've experienced mercy and justice:

JUSTICE   MERCY

Rainbows

What does God think of your sin?

God hates sin and, as the just Judge, must punish it. But God is also merciful <u>and has provided a way of salvation</u>.

—Q&A 6

A while ago a video surfaced on the Internet in which a guy saw two rainbows in the sky at the same time and began filming them. The video catches his voice as he gets more and more excited about what he is seeing—he describes it as a "double rainbow all the way!" At one point he is just so awestruck that he begins to cry and through his tears he exclaims, "What does it mean?" That's actually a pretty good question—what does it mean?

You would think that after being saved from the flood that destroyed the earth, Noah would be convinced that God would provide for him and his family. The flood was pretty horrible. Noah needed something to help him really believe that things wouldn't keep falling apart. I guess maybe we do too. God sent a rainbow as a sign of the covenant (promise) God made with Noah and with all of creation.

Jesus says, "I am the way and the truth and the life" (John 14:6). God fulfilled his promise to Noah and his descendants by providing Jesus as the way of salvation. God knew that Noah and his descendants (us!) would need a sign of his promise. He knew how quickly we forget about God, and that even though we have lots of evidence that God provides for us, we still need reminders. I know I do.

THINK ABOUT IT TALK ABOUT IT

When have you been reminded of God's promises?

So whenever I see a rainbow I try to remember what it means. Not only that God won't send a flood again, but that God provides much more than safety and food—he provides a way of salvation. That guy who got really excited about the double rainbow was on to something!

CHALLENGE

GOD SAVED US!

Look for "rainbow moments" this week—times when God reminds you of his love. Make a list here.

Jesus' Baptism

Read Matthew 3:11-17.

Imagine that you are coaching a pro football team. You know a few things about football, but you keep telling your team, "Start by doing this, but pretty soon Don Shula (he's the coach with the best record in the NFL) will be here. When he arrives, he'll make us into a championship team."

Sure enough, after weeks of practice, Don Shula shows up. Relieved, you run up to him, excited to get started. But he tells you to keep on coaching because he has other stuff to do. What?! You're Don Shula! We've been waiting for you! Jesus is certainly more than a good football coach, but I wonder if John the Baptist felt like that when Jesus told him that he had a different plan.

As John the Baptist preached repentance, he spoke about one who is more powerful than him, who would come after him to baptize with the Holy Spirit and with fire. But when Jesus did come, he was baptized by John—and then he left John to continue his work. Why?

Jesus knew that he had other things to accomplish. His next stop was a forty-day trip to the desert where he was tempted by the devil. It's easy for us to think Jesus really doesn't know what it's like to face the kind of temptations we face, but this story tells us that he does.

Each one of us has certain things that really tempt us, and the devil pulled out all the stops to figure out what would tempt Jesus. How did Jesus respond? He refuted the devil by quoting the Old Testament to him.

Knowing what the Bible says is a key strategy for defeating temptation. Just as John the Baptist was preparing the way for Jesus, Jesus prepared a way for us. John pointed to Jesus, and Jesus shows us how to live the best life possible. Now *that's* excellent coaching.

NOTE

IF YOU HATE SPORTS, THINK OF ANOTHER "COACH" SITUATION, — TEACHER, BAND DIRECTOR, DANCE INSTRUCTOR...

I'M OFTEN TEMPTED BY:

THINK ABOUT IT   TALK ABOUT IT

Jesus could have stayed at the river to baptize people, but instead he went to the desert to be tempted. Why did he choose to do that?

SPLISH SPLASH

CHALLENGE

Look up this week's memory Challenge verse, 1 John 1:9 and learn it. What does it mean to you?

WHAM!

BIBLE

TAKE THAT!

Your Baptism

"This is my son, whom I love; with him I am well pleased."
— Matthew 3:17

OOH THAT'S COLD!

Baptism can take many different forms. I was baptized as an infant with water on my forehead. Some people are baptized when they're older by being dunked completely underwater. No matter which way it happens, being baptized means the same thing: that you are a child of God, born sinful, and that God is able to wash those sins away with his grace. The water of baptism is a symbol that you're a washed person.

But baptism is more than a symbol. It's also a covenant, just like the covenant God made with Abraham, with Noah, and with Jacob. A covenant is like a contract—one person says "I'll do this" and the other person says, "OK, and I'll do this." We are baptized into the name of God the Father, God the Son, and God the Holy Spirit—all three persons of the Trinity are involved.

WILL BE R GOD, AND WILL BE Y PEOPLE

—GOD

God the Father extends the covenant he made with Abraham to us. We are surrounded by God's protection and are offered the saving grace only God can offer. Jesus the Son invites us to share in his death and resurrection, which is how God shows us forgiveness and love. The Holy Spirit assures us that God will live in us and helps us to follow Christ and to worship God.

Since covenants have two sides, when we're baptized, our parents and the members of our church pledge to help us learn about God and how to follow God. If we're baptized when we're older we promise to follow God—but the church still makes their pledge too.

Even though we're saved as individuals, this very important moment in our lives happens with all these other people playing an important part. We don't do faith on our own. We have the people of God surrounding us.

THINK ABOUT IT TALK ABOUT IT

CHALLENGE

DRAW A PICTURE OF HOW YOU IMAGINE YOUR BAPTISM:

Why do you think God chose baptism to be a sign of his covenant?

...k someone to tell you the ...ory of your baptism. Or, if ...u haven't been baptized, ...lk to a parent, mentor or ...iend about what baptism ...ould mean to you.

I've Got You Covered

SUPER FRIEND THAT **REALLY** SAVED ME!

Who can save you?

I cannot save myself. Only Jesus Christ can save me.

—Q&A 7

Q: *How does Jesus save you?*

A: *As a true human being, although without sin, and also true God, he was able to bear the guilt and punishment for the sin of all humanity.*

—Q&A 8

I didn't always do my homework. There were a few times when I had assignments due and I just didn't get around to doing them. It turns out that when you don't do it your grade goes down! I know—this seems totally unfair. But teachers are pretty relentless about stuff like that.

Sometimes I tried to talk my way out of it. I'm pretty good at that, but most of the time the teachers didn't buy my excuses. (Again, totally unfair. I worked hard on those excuses!)

What I really wished was that one of my friends would suddenly stand up, take out his assignment, and say "Oh, look! Here's Bryan's assignment! He must have dropped it." That would have been awesome. Of course, then my friend would have gotten in trouble for not doing his work, which would have made me feel bad. (I didn't have all the kinks worked out of that plan.)

This week's Q&A's tell us that Jesus is like that friend who jumps up and says, "Here it is— I've got him covered." Except that Jesus does it for more than just one assignment. In the "class" of life we don't do our assignments very well. We mess up all the time. But in our baptism Jesus says "I've got you covered." That's way better than someone doing my homework!

GEORGE WASHINGTON

THE END

WHAT? BUT THE PICTURE IS WORTH A THOUSAND WORDS!?!

LOOK! HERE IT IS!

←SUPER FRI

WOW! YOU REALLY SAVED ME!

THINK ABOUT IT   TALK ABOUT IT

How could Jesus bear all the guilt and punishment for our sins?

CHALLENGE

Jesus went the distance for you. This week show him love by paying it forward. Take time to help someone who is going through a hard time.

22

Covenant People

Where do you learn about this salvation in Jesus Christ?
From the Bible. It tells the story of God's saving acts throughout his covenant with Israel (Old Testament) and through the new covenant in Jesus Christ (New Testament).
—Q&A 9

ABRAHAM + SARAH

My roommate is a big Notre Dame fan. His grandfather played football for them, and my roommate and his brother attend as many Fighting Irish football games as they can. He displays his souvenirs and ticket stubs from past games in our dining room. This is a big part of his heritage, and he really enjoys talking about it. When you ask him about a game, he's happy to recap it for you. He'll tell you a lot more than you want to know.

ISAAC + REBEKAH

ESAU

JACOB + LEAH + RACHEL

The Israelites did the same thing with the stories of their heritage. In Exodus 24, God renewed his covenant with the Israelites, this time while Moses was their leader. This covenant was special because God was making it only with them. If you were an Ammonite or a Moabite you weren't part of the group. This group was for the children of Abraham, Isaac, and Jacob. Being a part of this chosen people was very important. So important that they kept track of who was in the family and therefore part of this covenant.

12 TRIBES OF ISRAEL (JUDAH)

The Old Testament is full of genealogies and stories of people who are in the line of David: Joseph, Ruth, the judges, and the kings. Through Jesus, though, the covenant was opened up to the whole world. To people like us! These stories are important to us because they bring us on a journey from the garden of Eden all the way to Jesus. They're our stories too!

THINK ABOUT IT / TALK ABOUT IT

Have you ever thought of the Bible's stories as *your* stories? How do those stories help make you who you are?

Knowing my roommate means knowing that he's a Fighting Irish fan. He makes sure of it. The stories he and his brother heard from his grandfather are a big part of who he is. The stories of our faith are just like that—they shape us into the people we are.

GRANDMA LOVES TO TALK ABOUT THE FARM WHERE SHE GREW UP.

DON'T GET ME STARTED!

CHALLENGE

...t your three ...vorite Bible stories ...order) and why you ...e them. Or, if you ...e to sketch, draw ...e scene here:

RECALL A STORY THAT'S PART OF YOUR FAMILY'S HERITAGE.

No Exaggerating

DO YOU EXAGGERATE BE HONEST.

Read Acts 8:26-40.

Sometimes when I tell a story I have a tendency to exaggerate. Recently we had a big snowstorm in Kalamazoo, Michigan, where I live. Everyone here is talking about how big the drifts are in their driveway. I heard someone today talk about a five-foot drift. Five feet of snow is a LOT of snow. Frankly, I've never seen a five-foot drift and I've lived in Michigan my whole life. When I hear stories about huge snowdrifts or the fish that got away, I don't always believe them.

This winter we had an ice storm in Kalamazoo. There was so much ice on the road that I put on my ice skates and skated down the road. Really. Really! You don't believe me? I had it videotaped just so I could prove it to you. Go to YouTube and search for "jonathanowenkraker13" on YouTube and then select "Ice Skating on the Road." That's me out there on the ice!

GOT GOSPEL?

YEP!

This brings me to the story of Philip and the Ethiopian. The story seems a little random. Why is it here? Why does it matter? Luke 24:47 says, "repentance for the forgiveness of sins will be preached in his name to all nations, beginning at Jerusalem." The concept of forgiveness for all nations was a new idea. The Israelites were the chosen people. How could this forgiveness be for all of the nations?

Merci!

Danke!

Ashi!

At the time of this story the Israelites thought Ethiopia was the southern edge of the earth. So an Ethiopian man receiving the good news literally meant that the gospel was stretching to the end of the earth! This story was like the YouTube proof to the readers that the good news of God's grace really is for everyone on earth! This was—and still is—a big deal. Because if God's grace is for everyone, that includes me—and you too. And that's no exaggeration!

THINK ABOUT IT   TALK ABOUT IT

Who are the Philips in your life? Who do you talk to when you have questions about God or the Bible?

CHALLENGE

Check out www.lastlanguagescampaign.org to see what Wycliffe is doing to bring the Bible to every language group. Click on a continent to see how many languages and how many Bible translations exist there.

A Covenant for All

This fall I went to see Part One of the seventh Harry Potter movie. I haven't been a big Harry Potter fan, but many of the youth group students I went with are. Before the movie, my students made sure that I knew everything I needed to know in order to enjoy it. They filled me in on what happened in the previous movies that I hadn't seen.

My sisters are also big Harry Potter fans. When the final book of the series came out, they went at midnight to buy the book and raced their way through the pages to find out how the story ended. They had waited years for this moment when they'd find out the climax of the story.

I wonder if the Israelites felt this way when they heard the good news of Jesus. We know that Jesus' death and resurrection isn't the end of the story—we're still living it out. But it certainly was the exciting climax. We also know how the story ends. Jesus said, "My Father's house has many rooms; if that were not so, would I have told you that I am going there to prepare a place for you?" (John 14:2).

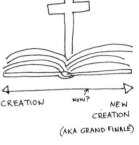

Jesus' death and resurrection are like a preview—it's like you've watched the previews of the final Harry Potter movie, you've bought your ticket, and now you're sitting in the theater with your popcorn and all your friends waiting for it to start. There's a lot of anticipation!

The real end of our story is when we are united with God in the new heavens and the new earth. While we are waiting, we can act like my youth group students (and like Philip) by sharing the story with all of our friends and inviting them to be a part of it with us. That's a finale I'm really looking forward to!

THINK ABOUT IT / TALK ABOUT IT

Do you look forward to meeting God in the new heavens and the new earth? What do you think that will be like?

TO BE CONTINUED!

CHALLENGE

Spend a few minutes praying for one or two people who may not know what Jesus has done for them. Ask God to make it possible for you to share a little about your faith with them this week.

THE FINALE WILL BE SWEET!

WOW, I CAN'T WAIT!

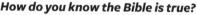

The Bible

All Scripture is God-breathed and is useful for teaching, rebuking, correcting and training in righteousness.
—*2 Timothy 3:16*

How do you know the Bible is true?
Because the Holy Spirit breathed into the authors, guiding them to write a true and completely reliable account of God's saving promises and acts. The same Spirit guided the church to choose which books to include in the Bible. And the same Spirit tells me, in my heart, that this is the true Word of God.
—*Q&A 10*

How does the Spirit work in you when you read the Bible?

When I was younger, my parents and teachers told me that the Bible was "God-breathed"—it was written with the prompting of the Holy Spirit through people on earth. I wasn't sure what "God-breathed" meant but I had a picture in my head of some guy in a secret dark room listening for what God told him to write. Now I realize that my view of the Bible wasn't big enough.

I knew that the Bible is a collection of stories, some of them really cool stories, stories that I enjoyed hearing as I grew up, and that I enjoy telling now as a youth leader. But now I realize that the Bible is really one big story—kind of like how there are six Star Wars movies, but together they tell one big story. Of course, there are differences between the Bible and Star Wars.

WHAT'S YOUR FAVORITE CAMPFIRE STORY?

One difference is that the stories in the Bible actually happened. Another is that one guy (George Lucas) came up with the idea for all the Star Wars movies and wrote them down. The stories in the Old Testament started verbally. The Israelites told the stories of God's faithfulness from generation to generation—the way we tell stories around the campfire today or the way you hear about what your Uncle Henry did when he was younger. Over time people started to write them down.

The picture I had when I was young wasn't completely wrong—the Holy Spirit was certainly at work in the writing of Scripture. But the Spirit didn't just work in a dark room with one author. The Spirit worked through the nation of Israel for thousands of years to give us the Bible. My guy in the dark room was kind of mysterious and cool. But I like the image of many people being moved by the Holy Spirit to bring me these words even more. And what's really cool is that when I read the Bible, the Spirit is working in me too!

Ask an older family member to tell you a story about something that happened when he or she was your age.

History

WHAT STORIES HAVE YOU HEARD OVER AND OVER AGAIN?

What do you read in these books?

All about God's mighty, saving acts as told in the story of our creation, fall, and redemption.

—Q&A 12

THINK ABOUT IT   TALK ABOUT IT

The church is our spiritual family. Who do you feel connected with at church? Who would you like to get to know better?

My parents grew up in different parts of the country. My dad is from New Jersey and my mom is from Michigan. They met in college and got married soon after. I know all this because they told me the story. I've heard quite a few stories about when they were younger. (To tell you the truth, some of these stories can be a little boring.) But as I get older I am glad I've heard them. They help me know my parents better—and it turns out that their story is part of my story too. It's not just history—it's *my* history.

The history of the Israelites was important to them too. They especially paid attention to the history of the covenant God made with Abraham. In that covenant, God told Abraham that he would "make nations of you, and Kings will come from you." This covenant was renewed through the prophesies of Isaiah, who wrote: "A shoot will come up from the stump of Jesse; from his roots a Branch will bear fruit." That "shoot" was Jesus.

It was important that Jesus, our Savior, came from the line of Abraham, Jesse, and David—just as God promised. The historical books (starting with Joshua and going all the way through the book of Esther) tell the stories of Abraham's children and grandchildren. They tell how King David came from that line of children, and then how other kings (David's children and grandchildren) followed. They tell how, even though the royal line stopped being kings on earth, one of those grandkids became a King who would rule forever—Jesus.

7,246,007...
7,246,008...
7,246,009...

These stories are a lot like the stories I hear from my parents. They tell me about who my spiritual ancestors are so I get to know them better. Because of Jesus, I am now one of those children of Abraham. So it's not just history—it's *my* history. It's yours too.

CHALLENGE

Make a list of all the places in the world you have family members (or people who are like family to you). Think about how God has guided and protected your family.

Songs and Psalms

THINK ABOUT IT   TALK ABOUT IT

What is your favorite church song? Does your family have any important songs or poems?

For my grandpa's funeral my sister read a poem she had written. The poem included things we remembered about our grandpa. This poem is special to our family because it expresses something important to us. We have special songs too. Whenever I sing "In Christ Alone" in church, I remember singing it at my grandpa's funeral. That song and that event are tied together in my mind. I have lots of happy song memories too. Every time a member of my family has a birthday, my dad plays "Birthday" by the Beatles. He usually plays it loud too. Sometimes he even dances—that part isn't pretty.

The Israelites had songs and poems that were important for different events, and they sometimes used them to remember things that had happened. Many of these are in the book of Psalms. Some of the psalms have headings that tell what they might have been written for.

Some psalms, like Psalm 100, which is a joyful song of praise to God, are happy. I imagine that the Israelites sang and played it loud, like my dad does with the birthday song. Some are not so happy. There are psalms that talk about how it feels when you are sad or angry. Some of them remind us of things, like the song "In Christ Alone" reminds me of God's faithfulness in my grandpa's life. Other psalms describe disappointment with God.

Even though the Bible is one big story, that doesn't mean that all the books are the same. Besides the law and the historical books there are psalms, proverbs, and a Song of Songs that shows us that God doesn't just want to tell us his story but he also cares about how we feel. Take some time to look at a couple of chapters in these books and see for yourself.

THEY SAY IT'S YOUR BIRTHDAY...

MY DAD DANCING

CHALLENGE

Create a short song or poem that expresses your thoughts about God. Don't worry; it doesn't have to be perfect. It's just between you and God.

It's a Deal

How did God bring us salvation?
Through gracious covenant promises given to Adam and Eve in the garden, to Noah and his family, to Abraham and his children, to Moses and the people of Israel, and to all people of every nation—through his new covenant in Jesus Christ.

—Q&A 13

What are these covenant promises?
I will be your God, and your children's God, if you keep my covenant, serve me alone, and trust in my saving love in Jesus Christ.

—Q&A 14

After I got my driver's license, my parents gave me a curfew. If I was late, they would move the curfew earlier. We had a light in the hallway that I had to turn off when I got in. My parents could see that light from their bedroom so they knew when I got home.

We make these sorts of agreements with our parents and friends all the time. We know what we have to do, and we know the consequences if we don't follow the terms. After God created Adam and Eve, he made a similar agreement with them. We call that agreement a covenant.

CHALLENGE

God told Adam, "You can eat from any tree in the garden except for one tree. You must not eat from the tree of the knowledge of good and evil. If you eat the fruit of that tree you will die." Adam could have anything in the garden—all he had to do was obey God's rule about that one tree. This is just like the deal I made with my parents; I could use the car but I had to be home by a certain time. The consequence for me not keeping up my end of the deal was an earlier curfew. Adam and Eve's consequence was much more serious: death.

This story takes a turn for the worse. Adam and Eve didn't keep the one rule that God gave them. Sadly, we've followed in their footsteps. Like them, we suffer the consequences of our sin.

I hate stories with bad endings, so I'm glad this isn't where the story ends. A little further along in Scripture we find out that God made new covenants with Noah, with Abraham, and with you and me.

We call God's covenant 'gracious' because we can't fully keep our part of the deal. We're not perfect. Spend a few minutes thinking God for sending Jesus so that we could be included in the covenant.

What are some of your household rules? Do you think they are good ones? What happens if you break them?

TICK TICK TICK

OFF LIMITS!

FREE FOOD!

YUMMY FRUIT!

Covenant: Noah

Earlier I shared a story of when I threw sticks at cars from behind a leaf pile. After I was caught, I knew I had it coming. My mom lectured me on responsibility and grounded me. I had to deal with the consequences. Although my mom knew I was young and made mistakes, I still had to face the consequences of those mistakes. I guess that's how we learn.

My mom could simply have said, "Bryan messed up. I give up." Instead she thought, "There's still hope. Maybe I can fix him." I'm glad my mother didn't take the first option. I imagine there are still days when she thinks, "There's still hope, maybe I can fix him" when I do stupid things.

It's a bit like what happened in the story of the flood. John Piper, a well-known preacher and writer, said we can see three important things in the story of the flood. First, that humankind is sinful. Second, that God is just. Third, that God still has hope for humankind and has a plan to fix our sinful nature.

Sounds kind of like my mom, right? When she caught me throwing sticks at cars, she was disappointed, she knew she had to punish me, and she had a plan to help me learn responsibility.

My mother's plan was just right for me. I no longer throw sticks at cars. God's plan is even better.

How does it feel to know that God's not going to give up on you?

Spend five minutes today dreaming about your future. What do you think God hopes and dreams for you? What plans do you think God has for you?

Covenant: Abraham

I will establish my covenant as an everlasting covenant between me and you and your descendants after you for the generations to come, to be your God and the God of your descendants after you.

—Genesis 17:7

Once, during middle school youth group, we split into two teams and competed for candy bars. Only the team that won got the candy bars. After the winners were halfway through eating their prize, the leader spoke up and revealed that she actually had brought candy bars for everyone. She proceeded to give the candy to the losing team as well.

I was on the losing team, so at first I was disappointed that I didn't get a candy bar. Not only that, but my team had to watch as our friends ate their candy in front of us. When we found out the losing team got the prize too, we celebrated! But the winning team didn't think that was very fair. They said they worked hard to win the prize. They weren't sure we deserved it. But soon they got over it and were glad to see their friends enjoying the candy bars with them.

When God made his covenant with Abraham, he promised to be the God of Abraham's children—and there were going to be lots of them. I don't know if any people who weren't in Abraham's family knew about this promise, but if they did, I wonder if they were upset that they weren't included. Later on in the story we see that the covenant with Abraham was fulfilled through Jesus' death and resurrection. And just like the candy bars in middle school, the covenant was then given to Abraham's descendants *and* to everyone else. The good news of Jesus Christ is for all people!

Imagine if one of your friends had won one of those candy bars and ran up to you, all smiles, saying, "One of these candy bars is for you too!" I wonder what it would look like if we shared the good news of Jesus like that.

WHAT IS YOUR *FAVORITE* CANDY BAR?

THINK ABOUT IT / TALK ABOUT IT

You didn't do anything to earn or deserve God's love... and you can't do anything to lose it. Do you believe that?

WHO TOLD YOU ABOUT JESUS' LOVE? YOUR FAMILY? A FRIEND?

CHALLENGE

This week, share this good news with someone: say, "God loves me, and he loves you too!"

Covenant: Renewed

Read Genesis 20:1-21.

Do your parents have a thing they say whenever you are leaving the house, or whenever they are dropping you off somewhere? My mom always says, "Bryan, don't do anything stupid." She still says that to me and I'm an adult! Most of the time, it worked. I didn't do stupid things. But every once in a while I would get into trouble, and she would have to sit me down and make sure I understood what "stupid things" were.

God had made a covenant with Adam and Eve, with Noah and his family, and with Abraham. Now God was renewing his covenant with Moses and the people of Israel. Up to this point the covenant had been kind of general, but there came a time when God had to actually lay out what he meant. Like my mom, he had to define what "stupid things" were for his children. God gave them rules to follow so they'd know what they were supposed to do. Those rules are called the Ten Commandments.

We learned through the story of Noah that sin deserves a punishment, but we also learned that God had a plan to fix our sinful nature. Part of that plan was for God to be very clear about what his expectations were. Over and over again, the Israelites messed up, but despite their disobedience, God remained faithful to them.

When my parents had to punish me for doing "stupid things," they always reminded me that they were still rooting for me, that they loved me despite my disobedience. In exactly the same way God assures the Israelites—and us too—by saying "I am the Lord your God." God is rooting for us, and loves us despite our disobedience.

What is your attitude toward rules? Do you feel the urge to rebel against them, or do you tend to agree that they're for your own good?

THE RULES

LOVE GOD

LOVE OTHERS

CHALLENGE

Talk this over with a Christian friend or family member: Why does God care what we do? Won't God just forgive us anyway?

Covenant: No Other Gods

~BEEP~
~BEEP~
~BEEP~

The first four commandments deal with our relationship with God.

- Have no other gods before me.
- Have no idols.
- Do not misuse the name of the Lord.
- Keep the Sabbath holy.

These four commandments tell us how to honor God. In reading them I think of geese. Recently my roommate and I started goose hunting on Mondays. He's a youth pastor too, so Monday is a day off for both of us.

Jonathan and I wake up at 3:30 in the morning so we can make the drive to a farm not too far from where we live where geese like to hang out. We want to be there by 5:30 in order to make sure we get a good place to hunt. In order to fool the geese into coming close enough that we can shoot them we need to get set up in the field before the sunrise. And get this—goose-hunting season is in the winter so it's often really cold. My dad and mom (and my sisters too, now that I think about it) all think I'm crazy. It's cold and snowy and early and I want to go and sit there quietly waiting for geese.

But here's the really weird thing: my church service starts at 9:30 on Sunday mornings, and sometimes I find myself irritated that I have to get up that early on Sundays for church. Do you ever feel that way?

I'm willing to get out of bed at 3:30 a.m. to go and sit outside in the cold of winter waiting for a couple of birds, but I struggle to get up at 8:30 for church. When I think about those first four commandments I wonder if this is one way that I struggle with having idols. Singer Keith Green once wrote, "Jesus rose from the grave and you, you can't even get out of bed." Ouch.

I HOPE BRYAN IS SLEEPING IN TODAY.

Is there anything in your life that you can identify as an idol? A boyfriend or girlfriend? A sport? A hobby like hunting, snowboarding, video games, or shopping? How can we change our priorities to make sure we honor God by not having any gods or idols in our lives?

THINK ABOUT IT TALK ABOUT IT

How can you tell when something that otherwise might be good (like a friendship or a hobby) has become an idol in your life?

CHALLENGE

We usually think an idol is a gold statue, but can it be a goose? Or a video game? Draw something that could become an idol in your life.

Covenant: Life Jacket

Last time we looked at the first four commandments. They helped us think about how we treat God. The next six deal with how we interact with others:

- Honor your father and mother.
- Do not murder.
- Do not commit adultery.
- Do not steal.
- Do not lie.
- Do not covet.

Have you ever been to a community pool and read the sign that says "pool rules"? It says things like "no diving, no running, no food or drink, no horseplay." I remember reading those and thinking, "That's no fun. All we can do is stand in the shallow end!" I wanted to do everything the rules said I couldn't: dive, run, eat, and play chicken with my friends.

Then I became a lifeguard and I was responsible for the lives of the people swimming. I changed my mind about a lot of those rules. One summer, when I was lifeguarding at a summer camp, a girl was in a rowboat about 50 yards from my guard stand out in the lake. Her flip-flop fell out of the boat and as she reached to grab it, she fell into the water. I ran down the dock and jumped into the lake as she shouted for help. I swam to the girl, who was wearing a life jacket, and pulled her to shore. (I hope you're imagining heroic-type music playing in the background as you read this—it was awesome.)

One of the rules of our waterfront was that if you were in any sort of boat, you had to wear a life jacket. This girl was not a great swimmer but by following the rules, she was saved by her life jacket (and, of course, the quick-thinking heroics of the brave young lifeguard). The life jacket didn't keep her from falling out of the boat, but it did keep her above water.

In life, we will have hardships. We will be tempted to covet others' belongings, to disobey our parents, to steal, to lie—basically we'll be tempted to do everything on the "do not" list above. But those commandments are like our life jacket. They keep us afloat. Fortunately we also have an amazing lifeguard—Jesus. But those rules are still pretty important. They show us how to live our lives in the best way, and they help us honor God too. How is *your* life jacket doing?

Which of these commandments is the hardest for you to keep? Why do you think that is?

Choose one of these commandments to really focus on this week. Pray for God's help each day as you try your best to keep it.

34

Covenant: Extended

Who is included in God's covenant?

Those whom God, according to his eternal plan and purpose, chose out of fallen humankind to be his people in Jesus Christ.

—Q&A 15

The promise is for you and your children and for all who are far off—for all whom the Lord our God will call.

—Acts 2:39

When I was looking at scholarship applications for college, there were a lot of regulations, such as "Must have a 3.8 GPA or higher and be active in the community." They were looking for students who were excellent, for students who deserved the money they were giving away. So who was eligible for those scholarships? Kids who are at the top of their class, the best athletes, the ones who volunteer a lot.

That's not the way it is with God's covenant. Q&A 15 tells us that the covenant is for "those whom God . . . chose out of fallen humankind." God doesn't just choose the best candidates like the scholarship people do. He doesn't choose the people who live the best life, who give the most to charity, or who sing best in the church choir. He chooses sinners like you and me!

So how can we be included in this covenant? The catechism answers that one too. First, by hearing the gospel of Jesus Christ; second, by believing; and third "by being made new through the Holy Spirit's working."

Students who receive a scholarship want to do the best they can in order to keep their scholarship, whether that is performing in athletics or keeping up grades. But it is often more than that. They are motivated to do their best to show they are thankful for the scholarship! In much the same way, as Christians, the Holy Spirit fills us with a desire to thank God for the covenant he extended to us. We do this by living to glorify God. That's the interesting thing—the good things we do don't get us into the covenant, God does that all on his own. But by living according to God's commandments, we show God how thankful we are.

COVENANT QUALIFICATIONS:

THINK ABOUT IT — TALK ABOUT IT

How does it make you feel to know that God didn't choose you because of anything you did or can do?

CHALLENGE

List the top three ways you show your thanks to God for choosing you to be part of his family:

1.

2.

3.

INDUBITABLE!

LOOK OUT! IT'S A BIG WORD!

Wet Hair and Wedding Rings

SPLISH SPLASH

How are people included in God's covenant?
By hearing the gospel of Jesus Christ, by receiving the sign of baptism, and by being made new (regeneration), through the Holy Spirit's working in their hearts and lives.
—Q&A 16

There's that word *baptism* again. It keeps coming up. Is it really that big a deal? So your hair gets a little wet. Do we really need to be baptized in order to be saved?

Let me start out by saying that there are things about baptism that I don't yet understand. Actually, there are a lot of things about God that I don't yet understand (because God is much too big for me to really understand). But I know that in baptism something cool happens.

About a year ago two of my sisters got married. I don't know if you've ever been involved in a wedding, but the planning is crazy. I was glad that I was living on my own for a lot of it because, frankly, it was crazy at my parents' house. Part of the craziness was about picking out the wedding rings. Wedding rings are a big deal—you have to get something that both the bride and groom like because they're both going to be wearing them forever.

But wearing a wedding ring doesn't make you married. The wedding ring is a symbol of the commitment that a man and woman make to each other. When you are baptized, that water is a lot like a wedding ring. God places that water on you and says that you are his. But it's more than that. One of the old forms that pastors used to read when they did baptisms said that baptism was "a sign and a seal and an indubitable testimony that we have an eternal covenant with God." *Indubitable* is just a cool word, right? Try saying it. Lots of fun. But what's even cooler is the idea: Indubitable means that there is no doubt.

Baptism is a sign—like a wedding ring—but it is also a seal, like a promise. God makes an eternal covenant with us at baptism, and that means there is no doubt about his love.

THINK ABOUT IT   TALK ABOUT IT

What symbols do you wear to show where you belong? (Think school, church, sports team, clubs . . .) Why do you think God wanted to include a ~~seal~~ sign and seal with the covenant?

CHALLENGE

Find a symbol that reminds you of your baptism (maybe a blue marble or a water bottle). Carry it around with you this week.

Being Made New

How are people included in God's covenant?
By hearing the gospel of Jesus Christ, by receiving the sign of baptism, and by being made new (regeneration), through the Holy Spirit's working in their hearts and lives.
—*Q&A 16*

Last year, I bought a vintage moped. The moped was in bad shape. It was rusty and the lights didn't work. It didn't even run. But I was confident that I could restore it and make it run again. So I started working on it. I didn't know much about working on engines but, I figured, how hard could it be? I did some reading about engine repair and learned as much as I could about mopeds as I tried to figure out what the problem was.

Eventually I got it running! I started riding it around the block, and it quit. I was at the end of my block and had to push it back home. (I found out that mopeds are a lot harder to push than bicycles.) As time went on, though, I learned more about fixing it and the moped began running better. I got the lights fixed, sanded the rust away and rode around town, very proud of my project. I don't think I'll ever get it to look like it did when it was new, but each time I work on it, it gets a little bit closer.

Q&A 16 says we are included in God's covenant "by being made new through the Holy Spirit's working in [our] hearts and lives." When you are a Christian, you aren't immediately made new, but you are beginning a process of "being made new." This process takes time and effort; it takes learning and commitment.

But we have a lot of help. The Holy Spirit works in our lives. Reading the Bible, learning from fellow Christians, and doing our best to follow Jesus also regenerates us, that is, helps us become new. Just like my moped, we are a work in progress.

Whenever I finish working on a part of the moped, I celebrate by taking it for a ride. I usually ride to someone's house—a friend or a member of my youth group—and share the success. In the same way, we should celebrate the ongoing work of the Spirit in our rebuilding project. And you should get excited when one of your friends has a part that is looking a lot more like brand new.

VINTAGE:

(VIN´TIJ) -adj.

A NICE WAY OF SAYING "OLD"

THINK ABOUT IT / **TALK ABOUT IT**

What parts of your life do you hope God will help you make new?

CHALLENGE

Take a few minutes to take inventory. Jot down a few ways the Spirit has been working in your life to make you new. Think of a way to celebrate!

ZOOM!

He Knows Your Name

Jesus knows everything about you. There's no need to pretend with him or hide from him. How does that make you feel?

Talk to God today about something that's going on in your life. He already knows about it, so don't hold anything back.

Read John 4:1-26.

I love working on my moped, but what I like to do even more than that is ride my bicycle. I often go pretty far—once I did 200 miles in one day. This past summer, I was biking with my friend Jake on the Kal-Haven bike trail that goes from Kalamazoo to South Haven, Michigan. In the middle of our ride we came across a church group who was stopped on the trail. We stopped to see if they needed any help. They said they were just taking a break so we started chatting with them. Together we had a great idea to trick their friends who were farther down the trail. We asked them what their friends' names were so that when we caught up to them, we could call them by name.

We caught up to the three people and recognized them from the group's description. We started talking to them. We told them we were learning to be psychics and wanted to practice on them by guessing their names. My friend started by saying to one of them, "Hmm, I'm sensing it starts with a J—Jaaa—Jacob?" Jacob was blown away! Then it was my turn: "Is it . . . Nathan?" Nathan was amazed. The third one was "harder" but finally, with our combined psychic brainpower, we guessed the third person's name: Emily. Emily was astonished. We soon pedaled away without letting on that this was just a joke.

I wonder how the Samaritan woman felt when Jesus told her that he knew all about her, without ever meeting her. I wonder how it felt when she realized that it wasn't just a trick, but he was the one she had heard about—the Messiah. How would you react if you were the Samaritan woman that day?

Jake and I aren't really psychic, of course, but those three teenagers on the Kal-Haven Trail sure thought we were. I imagine that later on when their friends told them the whole story they weren't nearly as impressed with our psychic abilities as they were with our ability to pull it off with a straight face!

HELLO MY NAME IS

What Jesus did wasn't a trick. And he didn't just tell the woman what her name was. He offered her a new life and the promise of salvation. He offers that to you too—and he knows your name just like he knew hers. No trick.

Salvation for All

DRAW YOUR SCHOOL LOGO OR MASCOT HERE:

How does this salvation become your own?
Only by true faith in Jesus Christ.

—Q&A 17

This past weekend, I was at a high school basketball game of two local rivals. Although the lives of these students are very similar and their schools are just a couple miles apart, the rivalry runs deep. As the game went into overtime, emotions got more intense. Fans from both teams were standing up and cheering on their friends, hoping for a win. The team I was rooting for lost the game, but the fans of both teams wore their school colors with pride.

During Jesus' time on earth there was a bit of a rivalry as well—between the Jews, who worshiped in Jerusalem, and the Samaritans, who worshiped on a mountain in Samaria. One day, Jesus was coming through Samaria and he stopped to talk to a woman at a well (the woman whose name Jesus knew).

THINK ABOUT IT   TALK ABOUT IT

The Samaritan woman asked Jesus a question about worship. What question do you want to ask Jesus?

The woman asked him a question that got at the heart of the difference between Jews and Samaritans. She asked Jesus if the Jews were right, if people really did have to worship in Jerusalem. Jesus answered by telling her that the time was coming when she wouldn't have to be at the temple to worship—soon she would be able to worship in Spirit and truth!

Then Jesus said that the good news was for her too, and that no matter what she had done in the past, if she believed, she would be saved. This woman was on the opposite team. She was a Samaritan and Jesus was a Jew. The two usually cheered against each other, but in this case they ended up on the same side.

CHALLENGE

The gift of salvation isn't restricted to one nationality, church, denomination, or team—it's for everyone. It didn't matter which side of the rivalry the Samaritan woman was on because salvation is for all of us. As Q&A 17 tells us, the only team membership you need is "true faith in Jesus Christ."

Catholics, Baptists, Pentecostals, Presbyterians . . . sometimes it's easier to dwell on our differences than on our similarities. List as many things as you can think of that all Christians have in common.

Living Water

In February the college I attended celebrates homecoming. As part of the fun, there is an annual tradition of jumping into a hole in the ice of the frozen pond on campus. When February came and I found myself standing in line for the plunge, I jumped into the ice cold water and then hurried to get a warm shower. The water in this pond was not clean. It was mucky and dirty, with who-knows-what living in it.

A couple of years later, I spent a January afternoon in sunny Florida snorkeling in the freshwater springs of the Crystal River, hanging out with manatees. The water there was refreshing, clear, and beautiful.

In Jesus' time, one of the ways of collecting drinking water was from wells or cisterns—big open containers that catch rainwater. Some of these held standing water that could get pretty nasty after a while. They might have been more like the pond at the college than the river in Florida.

When Jesus asked the Samaritan woman for a drink, he didn't talk about the quality of the water in the cistern. Instead he talked about living water. He told her that if she would drink living water, she would never be thirsty again. I have been told that in this passage the Greek words used for "water" start out with the kind of stale nasty water I talked about earlier, but then when Jesus talks about living water it changes to a word meaning "a natural flowing fountain." The water he is referring to is the refreshment given by the Holy Spirit.

The Samaritan woman was so amazed by Jesus' words that she left her water jar behind to get more people to come and hear this good news. We can have this living water too. Swimming with manatees was fun, but drinking the water of eternal life with Jesus is much, much better!

What do you think Jesus meant when he told the Samaritan woman that with living water she'd never thirst again?

CHALLENGE

Jesus describes a relationship with him as having a stream of fresh water inside so you're never thirsty again. Create your own metaphor—how would you describe a relationship with Jesus?

Forgiveness of Sins

Read Mark 2:1-12.

In this story, a man who was paralyzed is lowered into a room where Jesus is teaching. Jesus sees the man and, because of his faith, tells him his sins are forgiven. When we read this story, we have a tendency to skip over this part, and focus on the healing and where Jesus says, "Take your mat and walk." That's the dramatic part—the man is healed. Everyone there can see that. It's a miracle!

But first we've got to understand the motives of the man and his friends. We can't see their motivation, but Jesus can. "Jesus saw his faith," the gospel says, and he told the man, "Your sins are forgiven." The man who was parazlyed was there to be healed so he could walk again, but he also knew he was a sinner and believed in Jesus' saving power. Jesus could see his heart.

Jesus then turns and answers the question that the teachers were all thinking but none were willing to say. To prove that he really is the Son of God, Jesus tells the man to "take his mat and walk."

Sure, the healing of a man who is paralyzed is significant. Imagine: this man, who could not walk, now can walk! But Jesus points out that the bigger issue is what's inside our hearts. The good news for this man—and the good news for us—is that Jesus has the power to heal us on the inside!

HEALED HEART

THINK ABOUT IT

TALK ABOUT IT

Jesus gave the man in this story more than he asked for— physical and spiritual healing. Can you think of a time when Jesus gave you more than you asked for?

CHALLENGE

Talk to God about an area of your life that needs healing.

BONUS CHALLENGE: Draw the friends tearing the roof off the building!

A Little Help from My Friends

For it is by grace you have been saved, through faith—and this is not from yourselves, it is the gift of God—not by works, so that no one can boast.

—Ephesians 2:8-9

My friend Ben is really handy. He can build just about anything and fix just about anything too. I know that whenever I have trouble with something around the house, I can count on Ben to come and help—no matter how big or small the project is. If I'm moving, he'll grab the trailer and help me load it up. If my water heater breaks, he'll come check it out.

The men who were friends with the man who was paralyzed were committed to helping their friend see Jesus. When they arrived, they found the house packed full with people, but they weren't about to fail in their quest. They devised a plan to go in through the roof—they'd do whatever it took to get their friend inside. I wonder how the man felt when his friends tore a hole in the roof in order to get him inside.

We don't always know exactly what we need, or what our friends need. But God does. We know that Jesus has the power to heal us and forgive our sins. So be ready to help others, like Ben helps me. Maybe this is how God plans to get them to Jesus.

What can you do to make sure your friends know the saving forgiveness of Jesus?

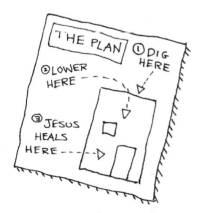

CHALLENGE

Spend some time praying for a few close friends. Lift up their physical and spiritual needs.

True Faith

What is true faith?
True faith is a sure knowledge of God's promises and a firm trust that all my sins are forgiven for Jesus' sake.

—Q&A 18

One of my favorite events in my church is celebrating the profession of faith of our members. (Some churches call it confirmation.) I get to hear stories of God's faithfulness in people's lives. Each time I hear a story like that it encourages me to keep trusting in Jesus—because God is faithful!

Sharing faith stories reminds me of a trust fall. You know, when you stand on a platform with a group of people ready to catch you. You have to fall backward without seeing what you're falling into. Ideally, you land comfortably in their arms. But this can be a nerve-wracking experience. It helps when the people who are supposed to be catching you shout words of encouragement like "We're ready, you can do it!"

Every time we share our faith, we are encouraging people, just the way we encourage someone to do a trust fall. Trusting God isn't always easy, but hearing the stories of others who have trusted God reminds us that God is faithful, and we can trust God too.

Do you have any stories like the man in Mark 2? Probably you don't know anyone who has been healed from paralysis, but I'm sure if you ask the Christians you know you'll hear plenty of stories about God's faithfulness in their lives.

THINK ABOUT IT TALK ABOUT IT

Have you professed your faith (or been confirmed)? If so, what did it mean to you? If not, is that something you want to do?

CHALLENGE

Ask a friend or family member to share a story of a time God worked in his or her life. Share a story of your own too.

"Humbled Himself"

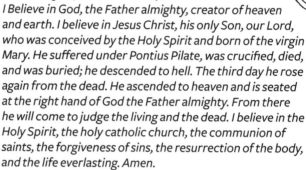

What do you, as a Christian, believe?

I Believe in God, the Father almighty, creator of heaven and earth. I believe in Jesus Christ, his only Son, our Lord, who was conceived by the Holy Spirit and born of the virgin Mary. He suffered under Pontius Pilate, was crucified, died, and was buried; he descended to hell. The third day he rose again from the dead. He ascended to heaven and is seated at the right hand of God the Father almighty. From there he will come to judge the living and the dead. I believe in the Holy Spirit, the holy catholic church, the communion of saints, the forgiveness of sins, the resurrection of the body, and the life everlasting. Amen.

—Q&A 19

Read Philippians 2:5-11.

What do you think it was like for Jesus to live a human life?

Sometimes I wonder if celebrities have to make their beds or do their own laundry. I don't picture Justin Bieber waking up in the morning and making his bed, or Miley Cyrus having to clean her room before she can hop on the plane to her next exotic destination. We just don't think of people like that having to do the things that regular people have to do.

Philippians 2 says that Jesus "humbled himself by becoming obedient to death." This is a big deal—God becoming one of us was a significant step down. It's hard to even imagine what it means for the almighty God to trade heaven for life on earth. More than that, Jesus voluntarily submitted himself to bear our sin through his death on the cross. It's shocking that he would do all that for us.

Think of some times when you've had the chance to humble yourself to show love to others—like watching Barney with your little sister even if you're way too old.

This week we begin to look at the part of the Q&A's that cover the Apostles' Creed—a summary of belief used by churches around the world. Most of the words in the creed tell the story of Jesus' birth, death, resurrection, and ascension. What made this story possible was Jesus' willingness to humble himself to be fully human.

It's hard to imagine Oprah doing the dishes or Lady Gaga folding her laundry. It's hard to imagine God doing chores, but he did. Jesus was willing to humble himself, to bear human suffering and even death because he loves you and me. Maybe I should spend less time trying to be like my favorite celebrity and more time trying to be like Jesus.

I Believe in God Almighty

Who is God?

God is one, spiritual being: eternal, invisible, almighty, infinite, and completely wise, just, and good. This one God exists from eternity in three distinct persons: Father, Son, and Holy Spirit.

—Q&A 20

GOD'S WISDOM

GOD'S JUSTICE

GOD'S GOODNESS

My roommate and I often talk about our day when we get home. I tell him about my work or about hanging out with friends, and he tells me about his life. I've heard a lot of stories about some of his friends and he's heard a lot of stories about my friends. We feel like we know each other's friends even if we haven't met them.

In the Bible we read stories about God and God's wisdom, justice, and goodness. And as we live our lives, we share stories with each other of the ways we have seen God in our lives, and we listen to the stories of other people's experiences. Slowly we learn more and more about God.

So far in our trip through the Q&A's, we have witnessed God's wisdom through the promises of his covenant. We have witnessed God's justice through the destruction of the flood and God's goodness through the sending of his Son, Jesus Christ.

Just as my roommate and I learn about each other's friends through the stories we share, we learn about God through stories too. We have to keep telling and listening to stories about God from the Bible and from each other's lives to get to know God better. Even the stories you know well are worth hearing again. Like a favorite movie or book, you appreciate something new each time you hear them.

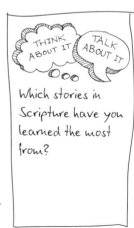

THINK ABOUT IT   TALK ABOUT IT

Which stories in Scripture have you learned the most from?

CHALLENGE

Fill in the blanks below with a story from your life.

I've seen God's justice in _____

God showed me his goodness when _____

I knew God was wise when _____

Father, Son, Spirit

THINK ABOUT IT   TALK ABOUT IT

Which part of the Trinity: God the Father, God the Son, or God the Holy Spirit, do you feel most closely connected to?

CHALLENGE

Make a sketch that illustrates the relationship between the Father, Son, and Holy Spirit. Then show how you fit into the picture.

Some people like to think of the Trinity—God the Father, God the Son, and God the Holy Spirit—as being like a family. That is pretty easy to imagine since God already uses family language like "son" and "father" to talk about himself. So if we think of the Trinity as being like a family (except without the typical arguing, rivalry, or being grounded) then we see three distinct persons called by one name, living together in community and unity, sharing all things and working for the same purpose. But this is no ordinary family. The Trinity is three persons, but just *one* God—very mysterious, right?

That leads to one of the coolest things about the Trinity: that all by himself God exists in community—one God relating as three persons. The whole idea of being connected to others, showing love, living in unity, practicing teamwork—all of that good stuff is part of who God is. We reflect God's image when we work together, share with one another, and show love.

Check it out: God the Father created and sustains all things, and through God the Son brings everything into existence. God the Son was sent by the Father to save the world and now continues to transform it through the power of the Holy Spirit. God the Holy Spirit awakens people to God's love and dwells within each of God's people, giving us gifts and power to carry out the mission of Christ—a mission to make all things new.

Each person of the Trinity shares in the family business of redeeming the world. And did you notice that we have a role to play too? That's because the Trinity of God embraces us in a giant group hug, inviting us to join the family. Not as part of God, but as a child of God, and part of God's world-transforming team!

North American Idols

Read Acts 17:16-34.

Let me tell you about a culture I've been reading about. The people there achieve status by wearing certain symbols; they put metal on their teeth and poke holes in their bodies to make them look more beautiful. They put badges on their clothes to show how important or how wealthy they are. They put their children in special places to try to help them learn how to make and manage money. They have a box in their home that they sit in front of most days for hours in silence. They spend hours posting pictures of themselves and letting others know what they are doing. It's an amazingly self-centered society.

DRAW A PICTURE OF A PERSON IN THE CRAZY CULTURE WE CALL HOME.

SOME NORTH AMERICAN IDOLS INCLUDE:

Sounds ridiculous, right? Until you realize that the culture I'm talking about is our North American culture.

I wonder if Paul came and visited one of our cities if he would say the same thing he said to the people of Athens? I wonder if he would be distressed to see a city full of idols. We may not have the same idols that the Athenians had, but we do have idols. I wonder if Paul would say: "In the past God overlooked such ignorance, but now he commands all people everywhere to repent. For he has set a day when he will judge the world with justice."

I'm not saying we need to burn every cool brand of clothing we own, or never wear earrings. But there will come a time when God will judge the world. So maybe we should spend more of our time worrying about the children who go to sleep every night hungry, or the families who don't have clean drinking water. I wish I could say, "My city follows Jesus." But my city isn't there yet. The only way I can change that is to change the way I live. How about you?

THINK ABOUT IT TALK ABOUT IT

If Paul were to visit your school, what idols might he find there?

CHALLENGE

Fill in these two lists:

Top 5 most important things/priorities in my life:

1
2
3
4
5

Top 5 ways that I spend my time:

1
2
3
4
5

Do your lists match?

Ignorance

I live about an hour from Lake Michigan. Once in a while we have guests from out of state who have never seen Lake Michigan, so we take them to see it. Those guests are usually astonished because the lake is so big that you can't see the other side at all. They hear the word "lake" and picture a small lake, one that you can see all the way across to the other shore. Lake Michigan is much bigger than that. It's like looking out on the ocean—all you see is water.

Paul calls the Athenians out for being ignorant about the gods they worship. They limit God by their temples, their images, and their idols. They put him into a box by creating images of gold, silver, and stone. They think God is very small. They invent multiple gods and expect to see them all at one glance, the way some people think they can see all of Lake Michigan by looking out at the distance.

But Paul tells them about the one true God. This is the God in whom "we live and move and have our being." This is a much bigger God than the Athenians were worshiping. They had gods that were so small that they knew everything about them. Our God is so big that we can't even imagine how great he really is.

THINK ABOUT IT / TALK ABOUT IT

How big is God in your mind? How would you describe God to someone who has never heard about him?

CHALLENGE

Daydream about how awesome God is. Consider taking a walk in nature, listening to a favorite worship song, or reading Psalm 8. Enjoy being with God.

"Wise, Just, and Good"

Who is God?

God is one, spiritual being: eternal, invisible, almighty, infinite and completely wise, just, and good. This one God exists from eternity in three distinct persons: Father, Son, and Holy Spirit.

—Q&A 20

"Wait Wait . . . Don't Tell Me" is a radio news quiz program. There's a panel of contestants as well as random listeners who call in. During the show a featured celebrity takes one of the quizzes involving multiple-choice questions. The person must get two out of three correct to win. If the contestant gets one wrong, the host often gives clues to help get the next one right. If the person starts guessing the wrong answer, he'll say something like "Really? You choose (b) the monkey with a tutu? You sure?" At that point the contestant will often change his or her answer to the correct one.

Most contestants could win the game if they just listened to the subtle (and sometimes not very subtle) hints from the host. The host extends grace to the contestants by helping them find the right answer. Sometimes the players are stubborn or aren't really paying attention to the hints, and they choose the monkey with a tutu anyway.

When have you felt God steering you in the right direction?

God extends grace to us the same way the host of that show does by helping us find the path to him. This path is through Jesus Christ. If we don't choose to believe in Jesus Christ, we become subject to God's justice. But God has a plan. God steers us to the right answer. He shows his goodness and grace by giving us three things:

- God's Word, the Bible, to teach us.
- God's Son, Jesus Christ, to save us.
- the Holy Spirit to guide us.

OK, not quite the same as a multiple choice quiz on the radio, but God extends grace to us all the same. Our loving God wants us to get the prize—eternal life!

CHALLENGE

Talk to God about what's happening lately in your life. Ask for help with any decisions you are making this week.

God Provides for Israel

Read Exodus 16.

I recently watched a video of someone who stepped onto an escalator thinking it was going up when it was really going down. The look on her face was hilarious. I like to think I'd never do something like that. But the thing is, I do things I would never want you to see on video! I bet you do too.

I thought about that when I read this story of manna and quail in the desert. God commanded the people of Israel not to take more than one day's worth of manna. But some people did take more, only to find it full of maggots in the morning. On the sixth day, the Lord commanded the people to take two days' worth of food and promised it wouldn't spoil on the day of rest. But some people didn't listen—and when they went out to gather manna on the seventh day, they found nothing.

I think, "Those stubborn Israelites! I would never do that. If God told me to take only what I needed, I would take only what I needed. If he told me to take two days' worth, I would take two days' worth!"

What have you been worrying about lately?

God gave the Israelites plenty of reasons to listen to and believe what he said. God brought them out of Egypt, out of slavery, and appeared to them in a cloud and in a pillar of fire. God took the oldest child from the Egyptians while sparing theirs. God took them safely across the Red Sea. Time and again God proved to be trustworthy. And yet they doubted God's Word—even when they had food every day. What were they thinking?!

But if I'm really honest, I have to admit that I'm just like the Israelites. God takes care of me the same way. I don't have a Red Sea story but I have other stories—like the time I survived a snowboarding fall with just a broken arm, or I got through a semester at college even though I was sick with mono. I wonder if people look at me the way I look at the Israelites. I wonder if they say, "Can you believe Bryan? God has taken care of him for years and yet he still worries about stuff." If they were looking at you, would they say the same thing?

Talk to God about something that has been worrying you.

God Provides for Us

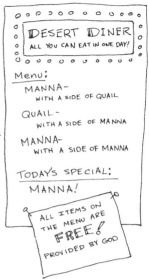

Read Psalm 124.

Here's a joke: Who had the best food in the Bible? The Israelites—because they spent forty years in the dessert. Get it? (I didn't say it was a funny joke!) I do wonder, though, about manna. Did they make things using manna as the main ingredient? Did they make manna waffles? Manna bagels? Ba-manna bread?

Seriously, God is a great provider. We see this in the story of the Israelites receiving manna and quail in the desert and in lots of other stories in the Old Testament. The manna and quail only sustained life on earth for one group of people—the Israelites—while they were in the desert. But God provides for us throughout eternity by offering his Son, Jesus Christ, to die for our sins so we can have life everlasting.

David writes in Psalm 124 about how wonderful God is and how much God cares for people. Imagine this: King David is sitting somewhere, maybe out in a field, observing the beauty of God's creation and reflecting on all the stories he has heard. The story of Noah and the ark, the story of Joseph and his brothers, the story of Moses and the Israelites crossing the Red Sea, the story of God providing manna in the desert. For David, these aren't just stories he heard in Sunday school; these are his family's stories.

When have you seen God provide for your needs?

David remembers all these things, and he is overwhelmed by God's goodness. He can't help but write a psalm of praise: "Our help is in the name of the LORD, the Maker of heaven and earth."

And David hasn't even heard the end of the story! Imagine David learning the ultimate story of God's providing—the story of Jesus dying and rising again to take away our sins. God does provide. He provided for generations of Israelites, and he provides for you and me today.

CHALLENGE

Write a psalm of your own (or compose a song) expressing your thoughts about how God has provided in your life. (If you get stuck, borrow some words from Psalm 124.)

GOD PROVIDES FOR US TOO:

THINK ABOUT IT **TALK ABOUT IT**

What are some of the ways God has provided for you today?

Tuition Money, Pizza, and Providence

Why do you say, "I believe in God the Father almighty, creator of heaven and earth"?

Because God is the almighty creator of heaven and earth and the eternal father of Jesus Christ. God is also my faithful Father, the one I can trust to provide whatever I need for body and soul.

—Q&A 21

Does God continue to care for the world he made (providence)?

We trust that our heavenly Father takes care of everything in our world.

—Q&A 22

Dear Mr. Keeley,

???

My parents tell a story of when I was just born. My mom had quit her job so she could care for my sisters and me. My dad was teaching middle school but he was also a graduate student going to school at night. Money was tight and they weren't really sure if they'd be able to pay the next tuition bill. A letter arrived in the mail from one of the parents at dad's school who didn't sign a name but gave them a bunch of money. I don't know exactly how much it was, but it was enough that they could afford for my dad to keep going to school.

CHALLENGE

Ask an older adult in your church neighborhood or family to tell you about a time that God provided for him or h[...]

I thought of that story when I read the story of the manna. God provided for my parents when they needed money to do the things God was calling them to do. Even though someone else put the envelope in the mail, they saw it also as God sending them the money. They actually have a couple of stories like that. A lot of people do.

MY FAVORITE

God provided for us in difficult times—just like he provided for the Israelites in the desert. It's easy to see how God provides when big things like this happen. But it's not so easy to think of God providing when I open my fridge and see some leftover pizza or when I go to my local coffee shop and have money to pay for a coffee. God also cares for us in the ordinary, everyday events of our lives.

Life Is Rough

Read Genesis 37:12-36 and Genesis 39.

We live in a broken and troubled world. Every day on the news we hear stories of countries at war or natural disasters taking out cities. People we love lose a job or face a bully at school. Parents split up.

It seemed that no matter what Joseph did, something bad happened. When he tried to be a good son and watch over his father's flocks, he was sold into slavery. When he worked his way up to an important position in Potiphar's house, he was wrongly accused of adultery and sent to jail. This didn't happen overnight, but over many years.

But Joseph had a dream. He dreamed that his sheaf of grain stood up straight and his brothers' bowed down to his. He dreamed that the sun, moon, and eleven stars were bowing down to him as well. This upset his brothers, but Joseph clung to the hope that someday it would be true.

Sometimes it feels like the whole world is against you or you're stuck in the middle of a mess. Maybe you didn't get the part in the school play or make the basketball team. Maybe things are tough at home or at school, and it seems like it will never end. This world sure is broken!

But God had a plan for Joseph, despite all the bad stuff he went through. Even when he was stuck in prison in a foreign land with no family and no friends, God was with him.

When have you felt like the world is against you?

CHALLENGE

Watch the news today and write down five ways you see the brokenness in your community:

1
2
3
4
5

Spend a few minutes praying about those things

God's Plan

How should you think about the troubles of the world?
I should trust that God rules and shapes what is happening in our world to his own purpose. The future is safe, because our world belongs to God.

—Q&A 23

Joseph gets called from jail to interpret Pharaoh's dreams. This is the big league; it's like having the President call you in for advice on how to do his job. Pharaoh is so impressed that . . . well, I'll let you read it yourself.

Read Genesis 41:41-57, Genesis 42:1-9, and Genesis 45:1-8.

What a turning point! This is the ultimate underdog story. Joseph comes out of slavery only to be put in jail. Then he becomes second in command over all of Egypt! On top of that, he is reunited with his family to save them from the famine. I wonder when Joseph looked back at everything that happened and realized that it was all part of God's plan.

When I was a young driver I got into a car accident. I didn't think it was my fault, so I was determined to take it to court and fight the ticket that I was given. On the day of my court date, my dad and I stopped in to visit my grandpa in the nursing home on our way to court. When we arrived, we found my grandma in the hallway. She told us that my grandpa was dying. We gave her a hug and went in to visit with my grandpa. He died that night, and that was the last visit I had with him.

I don't know if God planned that car accident just to put us at the nursing home that day or not. But knowing that an expensive and annoying accident allowed my dad and me the chance to be with my grandparents on that afternoon makes it all worth it. I was blown away by how God provided for me that day, even with the car accident.

It's easy to look back and see how God has provided through tough times. The hard part is trusting God to help you through the hard time you're facing right now.

THINK ABOUT IT TALK ABOUT IT

Is there a time in your life when God used something bad that happened (like my car accident) to let something good happen?

CHALLENGE

Today, when you face frustrations, take a deep breath and whisper, "God still has a plan!"

HI GRANDPA, IT'S ME, BRYA

Joseph's Job

Read Genesis 45:1-8 and Genesis 50:19-21.

Hindsight, people say, is 20/20. They mean that they can see the past perfectly—looking back, they see the things they should have done. The saying implies that we can't see the future or even the present nearly as clearly. Joseph experienced this 20/20 hindsight in his words to his brothers. "God intended it for good to accomplish what is now being done." But more than that, Joseph was patient, obedient, and faithful to his calling.

It would have been easy for Joseph to give up after being thrown in prison. The world was against him. Even though he tried to do everything right, nothing would go his way. This makes me think of the "teacher's pets" in every classroom. These kids are obedient and attentive, but their classmates mock them. They probably get pretty good grades and will be successful in their future work and life. Why? Because they make the right decisions even though they might get mocked for it.

Joseph was his father's favorite. He probably did all his chores without Jacob even asking. His brothers mocked him, plotted to kill him, and sold him into slavery. But Joseph remained faithful; he pursued God and continued to do what was right despite his terrible situation.

God is calling us to live like Joseph. No matter what the world throws our way, no matter what persecution or bondage we must go through, we are called to obey God and to follow after God's own heart. My prayer for you is that someday, like Joseph, you'll be able to look at the hardships of your life and say, "God intended it for good to accomplish what is now being done."

THINK ABOUT IT TALK ABOUT IT

In what ways do other people or situations make it tough for you to be faithful and obedient to God?

CHALLENGE

Spend a few minutes praying about the challenging situations you're facing.

Declaration

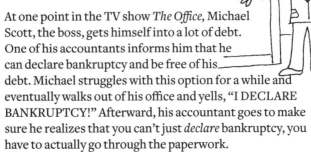

Read Matthew 16:13-17.

At one point in the TV show *The Office*, Michael Scott, the boss, gets himself into a lot of debt. One of his accountants informs him that he can declare bankruptcy and be free of his debt. Michael struggles with this option for a while and eventually walks out of his office and yells, "I DECLARE BANKRUPTCY!" Afterward, his accountant goes to make sure he realizes that you can't just *declare* bankruptcy, you have to actually go through the paperwork.

What does it mean to declare Jesus is Messiah through your actions?

In Matthew 16, Peter declares that Jesus is the Messiah, the Son of the living God. Jesus commends Peter for getting the answer right. Now, Peter doesn't have a spotless track record. Peter is the one who went to walk on the water but sank because of his lack of faith. Peter is the one who didn't want Jesus to wash his feet. Peter is the one who denied Jesus after he was arrested.

Peter was quick to declare Jesus as Lord, but his actions didn't always back up what he was saying. Just as Michael Scott can't just "declare" bankruptcy; Peter—and you and me—have to do more than just "declare" that Jesus is Lord. We also have to let Jesus be in charge of our lives.

We are all fallen creatures, and we mess up. A lot. We hurt others; we deny Jesus with our actions. That is part of being sinful. Peter walked with Jesus and talked to him, yet even he had trouble with these things. Declaring that Jesus is Lord is an important first step to living for Jesus. Asking for help comes next.

CHALLENGE

Talk to God about the times when your actions don't match your faith. Ask for help in living what you believe.

A Root in Dry Ground

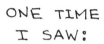

Read Isaiah 53:2-3.

Have you ever seen something that is completely out of place? Like someone on the beach wearing a winter coat? Maybe a guy downhill skiing in his bathing suit or a clown at a fancy restaurant? We remember things that stick out, things that are different.

ONE TIME I SAW:

Isaiah 53 says Jesus is like a root out of dry ground. Imagine you're in a desert. All you can see is sand dunes and blue sky. The hot sun is burning your skin. Then you look down and see a tender green shoot coming out of the ground. If you were walking through a lush forest, you wouldn't even notice this little green shoot. You might even step on it and never think about it again. But in the desert, you wonder how it got there. How is it living? You are tempted to pluck it from the ground just to marvel at it some more, but you leave it in hopes it will grow into something bigger.

Isaiah uses this image of the shoot coming from dry ground to predict the coming Messiah. But reading further, it turns out that the way people respond to Jesus is not like the way we might respond to a green plant in the desert. We will not, Isaiah says, marvel at his life, his beauty and majesty. Rather, we will despise and reject him.

That's not a very inviting picture. Being rejected and despised is worse than being ignored. The truth is, Jesus was despised, and still is, by many people. That doesn't mean he wasn't blessed by God. The Apostles' Creed puts this statement right at the beginning of the section about Jesus: "I believe in Jesus Christ, his only Son, our Lord." That our Lord would be born in a stable and suffer disgrace during his life is unexpected, like a root growing out of dry ground. But God often works in mysterious, unexpected ways.

THINK ABOUT IT / TALK ABOUT IT

Have you ever felt rejected or despised? Who rejected you, and why?
Does it make you feel any better to know that Jesus felt that way too, and he was God's own Son?

CHALLENGE Jesus came to a hurting, broken world to bring new life and hope. Pray for two people today who might be feeling rejected, despised, or ignored.

THINK ABOUT IT TALK ABOUT IT

When have you doubted whether God's way is really the best way?

Suffering

Why do you say, "I believe in Jesus Christ, his only Son, our Lord"?

Because Jesus Christ, God's eternal Son, is my only Savior from sin. He is my Lord who delivers me from Satan's power and makes me his very own.

—Q&A 24

Read Matthew 16:21-23.

I'm a Star Wars fan—can you tell by now? If you watch Star Wars in the order it was released, (starting with episodes 4, 5, and 6 and then moving on to 1, 2, and 3) you know that the villain Darth Vader used to be a guy named Anakin Skywalker. When you watch Episode 1, Anakin Skywalker hasn't become an evil villain yet. Even though you know how he's going to turn out, you learn to like the guy. You find yourself rooting for Anakin, even though you know the end of the story—you know he will become Darth Vader, the same character you rooted against in episodes 4-6. Weird.

GO ANAKIN!

WAIT, ISN'T HE A BAD GUY?

NO, YOU WON'T DIE!

GET BEHIND ME, SATAN!

Throughout Jesus' teachings, he refers to the Old Testament many times, sometimes even quoting passages directly. You have to believe that Jesus' disciples knew the Old Testament pretty well—just as many of their contemporaries did. Peter must have read Isaiah 53; he must have known the prophecy of Jesus' punishment because of our sin. So why didn't Peter see what was coming? Why did he try to rebuke Jesus when he predicted his death?

Peter, Peter. He was doing so well when he declared Jesus as the Messiah, but here he goes again thinking he knows best. Won't he ever learn?

CHALLENGE

Peter always says exactly what he's thinking (even when it means putting his foot in his mouth). Take a few minutes to tell God exactly what you're thinking. Be as honest as possible, then listen for how God speaks to your heart.

There are lots of times when we think we know better than God does. We don't get the chance to tell him that right to his face, like Peter does, but we sometimes pray it and we often think it—at least I do. Even when we know the end of the story like Peter did, we find ourselves wanting things to go our way, not God's way.

We can get caught up in what is going on right now, the same way we get caught up in rooting for Anakin Skywalker in Episode 1. God is in control and if he really is Lord (like we say he is in this week's Q&A's and in the Apostles' Creed) we have to believe that he knows what's best!

Separated

Read Genesis 28:10-22.

I consider myself a pretty tech-savvy person. I pride myself in my ability to fix electronics that aren't working right. The other day, I couldn't figure out why my TV sound wasn't working through my stereo. I checked the volume and made sure that both the TV and the stereo were turned on, but I still couldn't figure out why I wasn't hearing anything. The stereo is old and I thought that maybe it was broken so I gave up, disappointed that I might have to pay a lot for a new piece of equipment. A few days later I realized that the wires connecting my stereo to my TV were unplugged.

My TV and my stereo system work great with each other, but they must be connected in order to work properly. In order to fix the problem, I had to remember that my stereo and my TV are separate and they need something to bridge the gap between them—in this case, a wire.

We all experience a separation from God that began way back in the garden of Eden, when Adam and Eve chose to disobey God. Jacob dreamed there was a stairway between heaven and earth that bridged the gap between us and God. Sounds a little like my stereo situation, doesn't it?

In John 1:51 Jesus refers to Jacob's dream: "Very truly I tell you, you will see heaven open, and the angels of God ascending and descending on the Son of Man." Jesus saw himself in Jacob's dream; he is the ladder that connects heaven and earth! He is the only way we can be connected to God. What does that mean for you? –

THINK ABOUT IT TALK ABOUT IT

Why do you think Jesus chose a ladder to tell us about our relationship with God?

CHALLENGE

Talk this over with another Christian— maybe a parent, mentor, or pastor: With so many religions out there, how do you know that Jesus is the way to God?

Fully Human, Fully Divine

What do you mean when you say he "was conceived by the Holy Spirit and born of the virgin Mary"?
That the Holy Spirit made the virgin Mary pregnant. This means that her Son, Jesus, is both the eternal Son of God and a real human being.

—Q&A 25

What good does this do us?
Only someone who is truly God and truly human could become the go-between (mediator) who makes us right with God.

—Q&A 26

When did you first realize that you needed Jesus to connect you to God?

Let's think back to my stereo system and my TV. We covered the fact that they need a cable to connect them. But not just any cable—it has to have the right connectors. On my TV is a headphone jack, and on my stereo there are two plugs, a left and a right (these are called RCA phono jacks). In order to connect these two items, you need a cable with a headphone plug on one side, and RCA on the other side. Without this cable it's impossible to connect them.

So how does a cable cord relate to today's Q&A's? Jesus had to be two-in-one too, in order to accomplish his mission. Q&A 25 says that Jesus is both fully God and fully human. He is fully God because he has always existed as part of the Trinity with the Father and the Spirit. The amazing part is that Jesus is one of us too! He humbled himself by being conceived in Mary's womb and being born as a little baby, like every other human. The almighty infinite Son of God made himself very small so that he could enter our world both fully human and fully God.

Take a moment to thank God for sending the perfect mediator—the only one who could make you right with God.

Why did he do that? Because to be the go-between we need, Jesus had to be able to connect sinful humankind to a holy God. Only one who is fully human and fully God could make that relationship right by taking our sin and defeating it on the cross, and then offering us the righteousness that he has.

So Jesus is the perfect and only mediator between God and us. We can plug into that relationship by believing in the Lord Jesus Christ!

Mediator

Read John 1:43-51.

When I was in college, my sister was asked to play her viola with the band Jars of Clay when they came to town. My sister was excited and my family and I went to the show really excited to hear her play with them. She was great, by the way—she totally nailed the solo. After the show, we got to hang out with the band for a while and I remember thinking that these celebrities were surprisingly ordinary. There was no glow about them. They looked and acted just like average guys.

I wonder if Nathanael thought this about Jesus. Philip told Nathanael that they found the one Moses and the prophets wrote about—Jesus of Nazareth. Nathanael reacted with disbelief. He didn't believe that the Messiah could be from Nazareth. I wonder if Nathanael thought that the Messiah was going to be like a celebrity with stylish clothes and a winning smile. He didn't expect the Messiah to be so ordinary.

Many people were expecting the Messiah to be an earthly king, and to come into the world in a majestic way. But that wasn't the case. In fact, if Nathanael had remembered Isaiah 53 he might have known what to expect:

We often associate being human with being sinful—we say things like, "I'm only human"—but Jesus was fully human and wasn't sinful. What would that be like?

He had no beauty or majesty to attract us to him,
nothing in his appearance that we should desire him.
He was despised and rejected by mankind,
a man of suffering, and familiar with pain.
Like one from whom people hide their faces
he was despised, and we held him in low esteem.

CHALLENGE

The members of Jars of Clay weren't what I expected, either. Although once I thought about it, it seemed obvious—of course they're just guys. Jesus was not what Nathanael expected either, but he was exactly what Isaiah predicted in his prophecy. Jesus was fully human, just as he needed to be to relate to you and me.

Sin is only one of the things humans have in common. Make a list of fifteen other things humans have in common. These are ways that Jesus was like you and me too.

Justice

CONSEQUENCES

SOLUTION

What do you mean when you say he "suffered under Pontius Pilate"?

In his whole life and death on the cross, Christ suffered God's anger against sin, shown in Pilate's judgment. He suffered so that we might never suffer such severe judgment.

—Q&A 27

Remember when we talked about the story of Noah and the flood? There were at least three things this story tells us about God:

- God is just.
- God is merciful.
- God provides a way.

Let's build on those. In the story of the flood, God saw that the world was filled with sin and required justice. Romans 6:23 says that the consequence of sin is death, and that is what God brought in the flood.

Even with a new beginning, the world remained sinful and people remained separated from God. As time passed, the prophet Isaiah predicted that the Messiah would come to take on the final punishment that we deserved. Take a minute to read about it in Isaiah 53:4-9 and John 19:1-16.

The words of Isaiah came true in Jesus. Sin had to be punished because God is a just God. But this time, instead of people suffering the judgment for sin, Jesus suffered in our place. The anger God had toward our sin was directed at Jesus. Pretty heavy stuff.

I think sometimes we have a tendency to think of God merely as our BFF, full of love and grace. And he is. But God is also just. God can't simply turn the other way and pretend that sin didn't happen.

THINK ABOUT IT   TALK ABOUT IT

Do you think of God more as your BFF or as a just judge?

CHALLENGE

Sketch the picture of God that ~~you have~~ you have in your mind.

Just Love

Read Isaiah 53: 10-12.

J
E
S
U
S

HANK YOU

WE NEVER
HAVE TO FACE
HIS SUFFERING

Why does God love us this much?

One of my favorite Bible verses is John 3:16: "For God so loved the world that he gave his one and only Son …" This is a favorite of many people—and for good reason! It summarizes God's grace for us. I remember the night before I got my braces on when I was in middle school. I was so nervous I couldn't sleep at all. I was worried that it would hurt and that it wouldn't be worth it. I didn't see why I needed it. But my parents knew it was best for me. I'm sure it wasn't easy for them to see how nervous I was about getting braces. (I also don't think they really wanted to pay for them—braces are REALLY expensive!)

Isaiah says that it was the Lord's will to crush the Messiah and cause him to suffer. It was my parents' will that I get braces to straighten my teeth, but that doesn't mean they enjoyed watching my pain. They just knew it was necessary. Although it was God's will for Jesus to suffer and die, I'm sure God didn't enjoy it, but the Lord knew it was necessary.

"For God so loved the world." This is a deep love filled with commitment and sacrifice. The sacrifice was God's one and only Son. God sent Jesus to suffer the consequence of sin so that we wouldn't have to. Jesus is not only our mediator and go-between; he is also our substitute, suffering death so that we could avoid it. Now that isn't an easy love—but it's the best love!

CHALLENGE

Thank God for loving you with a deep, sacrificial love that cost so much. Ask God to help you love others even when it requires sacrifice.

OUCH!

OUCH!

BILL

HAVE YOU HAD BRACES? DON'T WORRY, IT'S REALLY NOT THAT BAD....

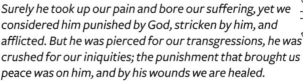

Substitute

Surely he took up our pain and bore our suffering, yet we considered him punished by God, stricken by him, and afflicted. But he was pierced for our transgressions, he was crushed for our iniquities; the punishment that brought us peace was on him, and by his wounds we are healed.

—Isaiah 53:4-5

In July of 1941 a prisoner in the Nazi concentration camp in Auschwitz, Poland, managed to escape. The guards reacted by choosing ten other people to kill in revenge. Franciszek Gajowniczek was one of the ten, but when he wept for his wife and children, a Franciscan priest named Maximilian Kolbe volunteered to take his place. Can you imagine how surprised Mr. Gajowniczek must have been?

The Nazis agreed to the substitution, and Father Kolbe was taken along with the others to an underground bunker and starved for more than a week before being killed by lethal injection at age 47. Mr. Galjowniczek survived Auschwitz along with his wife, though his two sons died there. Mr. Galjowniczek lived to be 94 years old—he lived 53 of those years after Father Kolbe had died in his place.

Jesus did the same thing for you and for me. But he didn't just spare our lives for this world; he saved us for all eternity! Jesus traded places with us to be pierced for our sins and crushed for our failures so that we could have peace with God. He is our substitute.

A year before he died, Franciszek Gajowniczek mentioned that "so long as he . . . has breath in his lungs, he would consider it his duty to tell people about the heroic act of love by Maximilian Kolbe." I wonder if you feel that way about Jesus?

THINK ABOUT IT   TALK ABOUT IT

How does it feel to know that you are off the hook—Jesus has taken all the guilt and punishment for your sins?

CHALLENGE

Talk to God about how it feels to have a substitute who took responsibility for all of your sin.

The King on a Cross

Why is it important to say he "was crucified, died, and was buried; he descended to hell"?

Because, by hanging on the cross, Jesus took on himself the curse of sin. He actually died and suffered the pains of hell. He did all this to free us from eternal death.

—Q&A 28

Read John 19:1-27.

This scene seems all wrong, doesn't it? It opens with torture as the guards flog Jesus and then mock him by twisting thorns into a cruel crown. They cover him with a purple robe and slap his face, shouting, "Hail, King of the Jews!" And I want to shout back "But he REALLY IS the King!"

We see a glimpse of Jesus' true kingship in his conversation with Pilate. He lets Pilate know who is really in control. Not long after, Pilate has a sign made that says, "Jesus of Nazareth, King of the Jews." I wonder if deep down Pilate knows this is true, or if he just wants to taunt the Jewish leaders. After all, their main charge against Jesus is that he "claims to be a King" (v. 12)—even though he REALLY IS the king!

Kings don't usually get mocked, beaten, and crucified. Kings don't carry crosses and wear bloody robes. Kings are the ones who have the authority to sentence others to death; Kings wipe out their enemies. Kings never have to suffer. But Q&A 28 emphasizes that Jesus allowed himself to be crucified. That Jesus "took on himself the curse of sin." Why? So that he could "free us from eternal death."

Jesus is a different kind of King. He rules with love and wins with sacrifice. He might have seemed like a victim when he was being tortured and crucified, but Jesus knew what he was doing. His death was his victory—through it he conquered sin and death. No other King could ever do that.

THINK ABOUT IT   TALK ABOUT IT

What does Jesus' way of being King tell you about power and victory?

CHALLENGE

Think of five things that only King Jesus can do. Spend a couple minutes praising him for the things on your list.

1
2
3
4
5

Hyssop

CLEANSE ME, OH LORD.

Read John 19:28-37.

Like every religious group, the Israelites had certain traditions—things that they did all the time that held special meaning for them.

In Leviticus 14, the Lord spoke to Moses and told him how to cleanse people who were unclean. Being unclean meant that you were isolated from the community and from God, so it was important for God to provide a solution. God told the Israelites they were to take the blood from a clean bird along with water and sprinkle it over someone with a hyssop branch. The hyssop branch was an important part of this ceremonial cleansing.

In Psalm 51, after King David had committed adultery, he confessed his sin to God and asked God to cleanse him with hyssop. We see hyssop once again in the story of Jesus' crucifixion and death. Jesus was on the cross and told those with him that he was thirsty. They took a sponge on a hyssop branch and held it up to his mouth so he could drink.

This makes for a cool symbol. The hyssop branch that was an important part of being cleansed in the Old Testament was now being replaced by the one who was sent to cleanse us from all of our sins for all eternity! We don't need the hyssop branch to cleanse us anymore, because we've been sprinkled clean with the blood of Jesus Christ (1 Peter 1:2).

SPRINKLED
≈ CLEAN ≈
WITH THE BLOOD
OF JESUS

THINK ABOUT IT
TALK ABOUT IT

Does sin ever leave you feeling dirty on the inside?

CHALLENGE

King David confessed his sin to God and received cleansing. Take a few minutes to confess your sins and receive the cleansing that Jesus offers.

Buried

Read John 19:38-42.

Why is it important to say he "was crucified, died, and was buried; he descended to hell"?
Because, by hanging on the cross, Jesus took on himself the curse of sin. He actually died and suffered the pains of hell. He did all this to free us from eternal death.

—Q&A 28

Recently, I've been watching a lot of TV shows about criminals and police catching criminals. Sometimes they solve these cases with just a couple of small pieces of evidence. The police and investigators spend days looking for evidence to prove who committed the crime. Then something the criminal didn't even think about ends up putting him or her in jail.

The story of Jesus' burial is brief, but it includes some very important details that were intentionally placed there to prove that Jesus was truly dead and buried. Criminals who were crucified were usually left on the cross for days to publicly humiliate them and make sure they were dead. Once they died, their bodies were taken to a shared tomb where they would find their final resting place.

Why is it so important that Jesus really did die?

But Jesus was taken with Pilate's permission from the cross soon after his death, so that he could be buried. The burial rituals of wrapping the body with spices and linens were done, and he was placed in a new tomb. This fulfilled the prophecy of Isaiah that he would be assigned a grave with the wicked (the tomb), and with the rich (the spices and wrapping) in his death.

Jesus' body was the first in the new tomb, his body was alone. This is important because when he was resurrected, the tomb was empty—completely empty! In other criminal tombs, many bodies would fill the tomb, but in this case the tomb was clearly empty.

Finally, the tomb was nearby. Everyone saw that he was buried there—no question, no tricks. The writers of the New Testament went out of their way to make that point very clear. Jesus was really dead.

CHALLENGE

Make a list of the evidence that Jesus really died and was buried.

1.

2.

3.

Conquered Sin and Death

Read John 20:1-18.

On July 20, 1969, millions of people around the world watched on TV and listened to the radio as astronauts Neil Armstrong and Edwin "Buzz" Aldrin Jr. stepped onto the surface of the moon. Everyone waited with eager anticipation, not knowing what would happen. It had never been done before.

I wonder if that's what it was like in heaven on Easter morning. I can picture all the angels tuning in at first dawn, eagerly waiting. I bet they gasped with awe when they saw Jesus, alive and full of glory, step out of the grave!

Jesus told the disciples that on the third day he would rise again from the dead. But they didn't really understand what he was talking about. How could they—it had never been done before! When Mary discovered the empty tomb and told the disciples, Peter and John ran there to see for themselves. What they saw puzzled them—grave clothes but no Jesus. The Bible says that John saw and believed; still, neither understood what was happening.

What they didn't realize was that Jesus' death on the cross was not the end of the story—it was the beginning of the victory! He had to rise in order to finish what he had started and defeat the enemy once and for all.

What do you find most amazing about Jesus' resurrection?

The resurrection is the most important event in our faith. If Jesus had stayed in the grave our sins would still be ours to deal with. If he hadn't risen from the dead then we wouldn't be able to rise again one day. Through the resurrection he conquered sin and death once and for all and opened up the way for us to have eternal life. Now that's a giant leap for mankind!

Spend a few quiet moments praising Jesus for defeating death and giving you new life.

Believe

Read John 20:19-31.

"Seeing is believing." That old saying means that we often trust our own eyes more than what other people tell us. In this story, it could be Thomas's motto.

Imagine the scene when Jesus appeared to his disciples. They were locked inside a room together, terrified of the people who had killed their master and wondering if they would be next.

Right there, right in the middle of their fear and confusion, Jesus appeared. He appeared as the risen Lord—the conqueror of death, with scars to prove it! He appeared to let them know that his death wasn't the end of the story. He is alive! "As the Father has sent me," he said, "I am sending you." And he breathed on them the Holy Spirit, the Comforter.

Poor Thomas missed out on this—and when the disciples told him they'd seen Jesus, he didn't believe them. I wonder if he thought it was just too good to be true. Or maybe he was too afraid or too sad to have any hope.

I'm glad that part is in the Bible, because there are times when I have fears and doubts too. But Jesus didn't give up on Thomas, and he won't give up on me or you. For Thomas, seeing was believing, but for us seeing isn't really an option. We have the stories of Scripture that tell us what other people saw. And when we believe, one day we'll see Jesus too.

> PEACE WITH YOU!

> THINK ABOUT IT / TALK ABOUT IT
>
> Do you usually need to see something for yourself to believe it?

CHALLENGE

Interview two or three Christians you know. Ask them what they do when they have doubts about something they believe.

> FOR ME, SMELLING IS BELIEVING!

THOMAS' DOG

Guaranteed Our Resurrection*

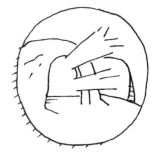

What good does it do us that he "rose again from the dead"?

By rising from the dead, Jesus conquered sin and death, won for us a new life, and guaranteed our glorious resurrection.

—Q&A 29

Which description of Jesus is most meaningful to you?

Let's look back at everything we've discovered about who Jesus is, because it's the combination of all of these things that, as Q&A 29 says, "guaranteed our glorious resurrection."

Jesus is our Mediator. Jesus is both fully human and fully God so that he can both take on the sins of the world and atone for the sins of the world. Jesus is our go-between and is the *only* way to God the Father.

Jesus is our Substitute. In Jesus' life and death, Jesus suffered God's anger against sin so that we would never suffer such a severe judgment. Our God is just, as seen in the story of the flood, but he also provides "a way" for us. That way is Jesus Christ.

CHALLENGE

Sketch a series of images that show Jesus in all of these roles (stick figures are fine).

Jesus is our Savior. Jesus took on the curse of sin and actually died, suffering the pains of hell, to free us from eternal death. Jesus died for the sins of the world, but most important, Jesus died for you! Just as the hyssop branch cleansed the unclean, Jesus cleanses us from our sin.

Jesus is risen. Jesus conquered death by rising from the dead. In the resurrection, Jesus won for us a new life. The new life Jesus was given, he shares with us.

Jesus showed his disciples, and us, that he is able to raise others from the dead too when he raised his friend Lazarus. So in all of these things, Jesus guarantees our glorious resurrection. Did you catch that? We are going to be resurrected too, so that we can live with Jesus in his kingdom!

Pleads for Us

What good does it do us that he "ascended to heaven and is seated at the right hand of God"?
At God's side in heaven, Jesus our brother pleads for us, leads his church, and sends his Spirit to pour out his gifts on us and defend us from all enemies.

—Q&A 30

Read Acts 1:9-11, 1 John 2:1-2, and John 10:29.

"It's not *what* you know, but *who* you know that counts." There is some truth to this saying. I'm a youth pastor at a church in Kalamazoo, Michigan, and before I worked here, I was a college student. When I applied for the job, I listed several references on my resume: my youth ministry professor from college, my boss from a part time job, and the director of a summer camp I worked for. These were people with important jobs and good reputations whose recommendation could go a long way on my behalf.

Not long after I applied, my professor told me that she had gotten a call from the church. She assured me that she'd given me a good recommendation. It was great to know she was behind me—and it must have helped. I got the job!

That's a little bit like what is going on in this Q&A. Jesus ascended to heaven where he rules at the right hand of God and pleads for us to the Father. It's almost like Jesus is our reference—except there is one big difference. When you apply for a job your references vouch for you. They assure the person who may hire you that you're a great person with lots of good qualities. But when Jesus pleads for us, he doesn't recommend us based on all the good things we do (our track records aren't that great). Because we belong to Jesus, he recommends us based on *his* perfect life and the forgiveness he won for us on the cross! When I mess up, Jesus pleads, "Father, forgive him—I paid for that sin."

THINK ABOUT IT   TALK ABOUT IT

What do you think Jesus is saying to the Father about you?

He does that for you, too. Jesus is on your side.

LIFE REPORT CARD
JESUS
~~~~ A+
~~~~ A+
~~~~ A+
~~~~ A+

LIFE REPORT CARD
ME
~~~~ D
~~~~ C
~~~~ B
~~~~ F

CHALLENGE

We can also plead to God for others. Spend a few minutes praying for people in your life who are hurting or who need the hope and forgiveness of Jesus.

Leads His Church

What good does it do us that he "ascended to heaven and is seated at the right hand of God"?

At God's side in heaven, Jesus our brother pleads for us, leads his church, and sends his Spirit to pour out his gifts on us and defend us from all enemies.

—Q&A 30

Read Revelation 1:9-18 and Colossians 1:18.

Last summer I rode my bike 200 miles across Michigan in one day to raise money for an organization called ActiveWater. This organization helps make it possible for people around the world to have access to clean water. After months of training, we were ready for our big ride—and I mean big—all the way from South Haven to Detroit.

We started at 5:00 in the morning before the sun came up, following a lead vehicle that had a map and GPS. The people leading the event had planned our course and knew every turn, road, and pit stop along the way. Another vehicle followed us to keep cars from hitting us (we were particularly thankful for them). We rode our bikes for fifteen hours that day. That was a lot of riding, but we didn't have to worry about where we were going. All we had to do was eat, drink, and ride. It was a great day.

Just as the lead van showed us where we needed to go, the glorified, exalted Jesus leads his church. As a cyclist, if I wanted to I could have turned onto a side street that looked like a fun place to ride or I could have stopped riding altogether. But I kept following the leaders because I trusted them to take us where we needed to go and I believed in the mission. I also knew that staying between those vans kept me safe.

Jesus is both our lead van and our trailing van—he unfailingly guides us on our journey and protects us along the way. Sometimes there may be a side street that looks easier or more scenic, but Jesus has a plan; he knows where we are going.

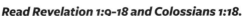

THINK ABOUT IT   **TALK ABOUT IT**

How does Jesus lead you? How can you tell when he's guiding you one way or another?

CHALLENGE

Find out how Jesus leads your church. Interview an elder or pastor this week to ask how the leaders listen to God as they make plans for the church. See if they can give you a few examples.

BONUS CHALLENGE:
Ask to videotape the interview and to post it on your church website.

Sends His Spirit

What good does it do us that he "ascended to heaven and is seated at the right hand of God"?

At God's side in heaven, Jesus our brother pleads for us, leads his church, and sends his Spirit to pour out his gifts on us and defend us from all enemies.

—Q&A 30

TEACHER

CHOIR DIRECTOR

Read 1 Corinthians 12:4-7.

In the show *Survivor*, two teams live on an island or somewhere in the wilderness with limited survival tools. The teams compete in challenges that have various components. Sometimes they require strength, sometimes strategy, sometimes problem-solving, and sometimes swimming or running.

The best teams on *Survivor* have players with a variety of skills. Some are good at puzzles, some are really strong, some are great runners, and some are good at strategizing. Together the team can solve problems, win a race, or lift heavy things. They can do it all. If everyone on the team is really strong but terrible at puzzles and all the rest, they won't get very far in the game at all!

The same is true in the church (minus the competition part). Jesus sends his Spirit to equip the church with various gifts that help us serve God together. 1 Corinthians 12:7 says, "Now to each one the manifestation of the Spirit is given for the common good."

In a church, some people may have the gift of music, others may have the gift of teaching, others leadership, service, cooking, or childcare. Each one of these gifts is given for the benefit of everyone, for the glory of God. If you have the gift of music, you are called to use that gift for the common good. If it is childcare, you are called to use that.

We don't have to worry about whether we have the best gifts or whether someone else does something better than we do. When we use all our gifts together as a team we can do great things for God's kingdom!

> THINK ABOUT IT   TALK ABOUT IT
>
> What special gifts have been given to you? How do you (or could you) use your gifts for the common good?

ON "SURVIVOR", WHAT WOULD YOUR SKILLS BE?

CHALLENGE — Think of (or sketch) three people in your church and the gifts you see in them:

Sheep and Goats

How does Christ's return "to judge the living and the dead" comfort you?

I know that my Savior will come as the Judge. He will condemn all his enemies and welcome me and all his chosen ones into the joy and glory of heaven.

—Q&A 31

Read Matthew 25:31-46.

When I was in elementary school our class went to the public pool for swimming lessons. We loved it because there were always ten minutes of free time at the end when you could do whatever you wanted. Go swimming during school? What could be better! But the very first day of swimming lessons was always stressful.

We would walk into the locker room and the instructor would judge our sizes and hand each person a swimsuit. The swimsuits were different colors: red was the smallest, then blue, and black was the biggest. It was always embarrassing for the students who got the black swimsuits.

After we changed into our swimsuits, we would line up and take turns swimming across the pool so that the instructor could judge our swimming ability and place us in swimming groups ranging from beginner to advanced—another opportunity for embarrassment. The only people who enjoyed this day were the skinny kids who were good swimmers.

I wonder if the final judgment day will be as uncomfortable as the first day of swimming lessons. There wasn't a thing any of my classmates could do about the color of suit they were handed. There probably wasn't a whole lot they could do about how good they were at swimming either. Kids who had pools at home or nearby were bound to be better swimmers.

The difference between swimming lessons and the final judgment is that we *can* do something about it. In the parable of the sheep and the goats, Jesus tells us pretty clearly what we have to do: love him, and love others. The way we treat people should be a reflection of our love for him. So he calls us to care for people who are lonely, hungry, or isolated.

BEST SWIMMERS STAND HERE

NO REALLY... THESE RED ONES FIT JUST FINE!

THIS IS SO HUMILIATING

WOR SWIMM STAND H

THINK ABOUT IT

TALK ABOUT IT

What do you find surprising in this story?

CHALLENGE

Draw a chart that shows how our relationship with God affects the way we treat others, and how the way we treat others affects our relationship with God.

Who Deserves It?

Read Matthew 18:21-35.

Last time we read the story of the sheep and the goats. Today's parable illustrates why Jesus is so serious about how we treat others. In this parable, a king forgives a large debt owed by one of his servants. The same servant goes out and has another servant thrown in jail because he owed him a small amount of money. Grace was shown to this servant, but he didn't show grace to others.

I have a similar story from my life. I've already mentioned that my twin sister and I shared a car in high school and college. We both felt entitled to the car. We would get into arguments about who should be able to use the car at any given time. Often we would bring the argument to our parents to let them settle it. Both of us were sure they would see it our way. One of my parents' favorite answers was "This is easy to decide. You're arguing about who will take our car. Keep arguing and nobody gets it." They were reminding us that we didn't own the car, they did.

My parents were right, of course. They were doing us a big favor letting us use the car, even if it meant we had to share it. By threatening to take it away, they reminded us that car privileges were a gift we shouldn't take for granted, and if they were willing to share their car with us, we should be willing to share it with each other.

This principle touches all of our relationships. We don't earn or deserve the love, forgiveness, and grace God gives us. But he gives it to us anyway. So we're called to show love, forgiveness and grace to others (who don't deserve it just as much as we don't deserve it). God thinks they should get it anyway.

> **THINK ABOUT IT** **TALK ABOUT IT**
>
> It seems fair for God to ask us to treat people the same way he's treated us. Why is it so hard?

CHALLENGE

Do a mental run-through of your words and actions toward others so far this week. Then spend a few minutes talking to God about it.

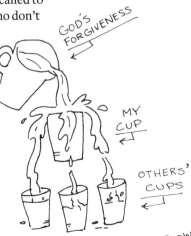

GOD'S FORGIVENESS

MY CUP

OTHERS' CUPS

DOES YOUR CUP OVERFLOW?

Enough to Go Around

Read Matthew 25:45.

At the church I work for, the congregation treats our staff very well. Often someone will stop by to give one of us a treat—cookies, cake, almost anything. You never know what you will find!

There is a common understanding that if one of us is blessed with a treat or snack, we share it with the others on staff. Although intended for one person, we all benefit, and whoever receives the treat is excited to share it with the others. It makes for a great work environment. We take our blessings and bless others with them.

Jesus wants to see that happen on a much larger scale. If my coworkers at church ate their whole cake in front of the rest of us without offering us any, we would consider that very rude. God has blessed many of us with plenty of food to eat, a roof over our head, clean water, schools, transportation, heat and air conditioning. But around our world and in our neighborhoods are some people who are homeless or hungry, who don't have clean water to drink, transportation, or good schools. Can we sit back and watch this happen without offering to share a piece of our blessing?

What is God calling you to share with others?

"Truly I tell you," Jesus says, "whatever you did not do for the least of these, you did not do for me."

CHALLENGE

Find out about hunger initiatives in your denomination and your community and get involved. Do some research online and ask your youth pastor what your church can do or is doing to help end local and global hunger.

WHAT HAS GOD BLESSED YOU WITH?

Anticipation

What is our great hope?

We long for the time when Jesus will return as triumphant King to rule the universe. Then we will live with him in the new creation.

—Q&A 32

Read Isaiah 35.

At my high school there's a tradition that the parents of the senior class throw an all-night party for the seniors on the night of graduation. The party is always at a special place that's kept secret until the big night.

At my graduation everyone was excited for the trip! We were told to pack a swimsuit, gym clothes, and street clothes. So we knew we would be at a place with a pool and a gym, but we didn't know any of the details—like what we would eat or what else would be there. We didn't know much, but we knew it would be fun. Finally the time came to board the bus and leave for the mystery location.

In my Bible, Isaiah 35 has the heading "Joy of the Redeemed." This passage gives us some clues about the new heaven and earth. It's a depiction of the time of redemption. The visuals are vague but important. It speaks of new life, healing, and redemption for both the earth and for the people in it.

All we know is the broken world we live in, so it's hard to imagine just how great the new heavens and the new earth will be. We won't fully know until we arrive!

THINK ABOUT IT   TALK ABOUT IT

Do you look forward to the new heavens and the new earth?

CHALLENGE   Use the description in Isaiah 35 to sketch a heavenly scene.

WHO KNOWS WHERE?

making All Things new

What is our great hope?

We long for the time when Jesus will return as triumphant king to rule the universe. Then we will live with him in the new creation.

—Q&A 32

Read Revelation 21:1-7.

Christians believe a lot of different things about what will happen when Jesus returns. Some imagine a day filled with panic, chaos, and fear as some people are snatched up to heaven and others are left behind. That's not what Q&A 32 says, and it's not the way Revelation 21:1-7 tells the story.

The day that Jesus returns is a day of great hope! There are at least three things to look forward to about that day:

- God's dwelling place will be among the people. We actually get to live with God!
- There will be no more death, mourning, or crying!
- Jesus will make everything new.

There's one more really great thing here. What comes down from heaven? A city! You might expect that God might want to go back to a peaceful, quiet garden, where it all began. But the new Jerusalem is a bustling, beautiful city, and that means that God isn't starting all over. The new earth includes human life, stuff that we've built. It will all be purified and made right, but it will be a city.

I love it that God will honor and use the stuff we've built in his new creation.

If Jesus is your Savior and the leader of your life, then his return is something you can look forward to. It will be the happiest day of your life!

THINK ABOUT IT   TALK ABOUT IT

What sounds best to you about the new heavens and the new earth?

CHALLENGE

Sketch the scene from Revelations 21:1-7. Be sure to put yourself inside it!

Reunited

Read John 14:1-6.

I'm excited about this upcoming weekend because my college roommate is coming back to Michigan to hang out. Two years ago Josh moved back home to Georgia, and we've stayed in touch but haven't seen much of each other since then. I'm sure our time will be filled with sharing stories about our lives and retelling the stories of our college days. When we lived together we learned a lot about each other.

When Josh moved back to Georgia, he told me he would come back to visit (and I knew he really would because his fiancée lives here too) but I didn't know exactly when he would visit. In the meantime, Josh and I have stayed in touch through Facebook and phone calls, but it isn't the same as being able to hang out together.

THINK ABOUT IT / TALK ABOUT IT

How do you stay in touch with Jesus?

Jesus told his disciples in John 14 that he was going to his father's house to prepare a place for them and that he would come back to take them there with him. Jesus also told them that they knew the way there. Thomas doesn't quite understand, so he objects, "Lord, we don't know where you are going, so how can we know the way?" Jesus replies, "I am the way, the truth, and the life."

Now we're waiting for Jesus too. In the meantime the Holy Spirit helps us stay in touch with Jesus. When we read his Word, pray, worship, serve others, and spend time with God's people, we can hear him speak to our hearts. But someday—maybe soon—we'll get to see him face to face.

CHALLENGE

Try a new way of connecting with Jesus, something you don't ordinarily do. Sing your prayer, take a walk with God, use art to share what's on your mind, read a psalm, sit quietly and listen for God, or work on a project that will bless someone else.

Given to Me Personally

DRAW YOUR FAMILY HERE

What do you believe about "the Holy Spirit"?
The Holy Spirit is eternal God. Given to me personally, the Spirit unites me with Jesus Christ, comforts me, and stays with me forever.

—Q&A 33

Read John 14:15-31.

Have you ever looked around at a family reunion and thought, "Who are all these people?!" You smile politely and shake hands as your mom says something like, "You remember Great-Aunt Ethel, don't you? And this is your third cousin twice removed." Then you share an awkward meal together and part ways until the next family reunion.

Sometimes we treat the Holy Spirit like a distant relative (rather than eternal God given to us personally). We think about the Holy Spirit once a year or so (around Pentecost), but after that we go back to our everyday lives and think a lot more about God the Father and God the Son. Even in the Apostles' Creed, we only give the Holy Spirit two lines, one in the long section about Jesus ("Who was conceived by the Holy Spirit") and then one other line: "I believe in the Holy Spirit."

What does it mean to you that the Holy Spirit is given to you personally? When have you sensed God's presence with you?

So how should we think of and relate to the Holy Spirit? If we read the next few lines of the creed, after "I believe in the Holy Spirit" we see "The holy catholic church, the communion of saints. . . ." This is where we see the Spirit at work—in our connections with our brothers and sisters in Christ. We can see the Spirit all around us through the faith of our parents and other older members of the church, the energy of young people, and the hope of children. The Holy Spirit is present in our worship, in our work, in our friendships, sports, games, and in our sleep.

The Holy Spirit is the one who wakes us up to the need for salvation through Jesus Christ, the one who unites us with Christ. The Holy Spirit lives in each of us who believe—binding us all together as the people of God, one family in Christ.

Write down three questions you have about the Holy Spirit. Spend a couple minutes praying those questions to God.

So maybe the Holy Spirit isn't like a distant relative after all. Maybe the Spirit is more like a parent or grandparent whose everyday love and presence is so comfortable and expected that we take it for granted.

Tongues of Fire

Read Acts 2:1-13.

In the United States the 4th of July is a day that many people love. It gives them a chance to go camping, get out the grills, spend time at the beach, and enjoy what is usually a warm summer afternoon. But the part I like best is the fireworks.

Last summer some friends and I decided to go camping over the 4th of July weekend. We packed up, found a campground that actually had an open spot, and hit the trail. At dusk on the 4th a group of guys gathered on the beach to show off their fireworks collection for their families.

We admired the show for a while, and then one of the guys asked us to help get ready for the grand finale. We agreed, pretty excited to be able to help light the giant fireworks. We lined up along the shoreline and lit all the fireworks at once. At first the display was glorious, loud and bright. Then a couple of the fireworks fell over and started launching into the crowd. Chaos broke out, and everyone ran away yelling and screaming. When the fireworks stopped everyone checked their tents and loved ones to make sure they were OK.

I wonder if this was what it was like for the disciples and the people watching on the first Pentecost. All of a sudden there was the sound of a violent wind, and they saw tongues of fire resting on each person's head. It must have been pretty startling. Everyone was filled with the Spirit and began to speak in tongues. I wonder if those people reacted the way people reacted to the fireworks at the 4th of July.

But being filled with the Spirit is much more exciting than runaway fireworks. These people were seeing the power of God the Holy Spirit breaking out right in their community. What do you think it was like?

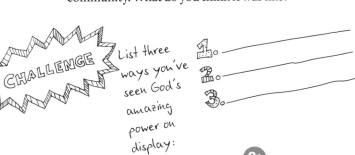

CHALLENGE — List three ways you've seen God's amazing power on display:

1. _____
2. _____
3. _____

THINK ABOUT IT · TALK ABOUT IT

Why do you think God chose fire to be a sign of the Holy Spirit?

Response

ZDRA...

おはよう

안녕하세...

... ...

MERNÈ

здравo

Read Acts 2:14-41.

There was a big crowd gathered on the first Pentecost. There was quite a commotion too. Each apostle was speaking in a different language, and the crowd that gathered understood what they were saying but couldn't make sense of what was happening. Finally Peter stood up to address the crowd and explain what they were seeing.

Peter started by quoting the prophet Joel. He explained that this was a different time: "the last days." He explained that God's Spirit had been poured out, and how all the things they were seeing had been prophesied. Most important he explained that all who call on the name of the Lord will be saved.

Peter ended by sharing the good news of the gospel. "Jesus is the Messiah," he said, "and Jesus was crucified for your sins." After the crowd heard this, the Bible says, "they were cut to the heart." They knew that what Peter said was true. They knew they had to do something, so they asked the apostles what they could do. Peter responded by saying, "Repent and believe."

The reaction of the crowd in this story really gets to me. I'm struck by the phrase "they were cut to the heart." It's not often that the good news of the gospel cuts to my heart. I know God loves me and that Jesus died for my sins, but that's just a fact I grew up with. I wonder if I should ache for God like those people did.

Then I realize that the way my heart aches for God is different than the way the crowd's hearts hurt. I know that God loves me, and there are times in worship— sometimes in church and sometimes on my own—when my heart turns to God in an emotional way. But my heart also hurts when I hear about a tsunami that leaves thousands dead and others without a home. My heart hurts when I hear about children dying from hunger or from thirst or from AIDS.

Whenever we are "cut to the heart" we can ask the same questions that the crowds asked the disciples: "What can we do?"

THINK ABOUT IT TALK ABOUT IT

We can be cut to the heart by our own sin and the brokenness we see in the world. What makes your heart ache? What can you do?

CHALLENGE

Make a list of all the things that you think break God's heart.

○
○
○
○
○
○

What is God doing about these things?

Sharing

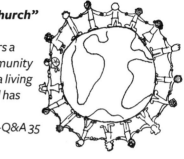

What do you believe about "the holy catholic church" and "the communion of saints"?

The Son of God, through his Spirit and Word, gathers a community out of the entire human race. This community is chosen for eternal life and united in true faith. As a living member of this community, I must use the gifts God has given me to serve him in the church and the world.

—*Q&A 35*

Read Acts 4:32-37.

Imagine that your whole church lived in the same neighborhood, with the church building in the center. Everybody who lived in the neighborhood was part of the church and shared everything they had with each other. Everyone worked in the neighborhood and kept all that they earned at the church. Nobody had to worry about money—if they needed something, they could get it.

Sounds like a pretty cool place to live, huh? You'd never have to worry about meals or money. You'd just live together in unity—with each person doing his or her part. *Unity* is an important word here—we are all *united* together in Christ. And by *all* I don't just mean the people in your home church—I mean the people in all the churches. That's the cool thing about this holy catholic church that the Apostles' Creed talks about. It's all of us. There are people in the farthest reaches of the world who are members of the church with me and with you.

Sadly, things get in the way of expressing our unity. Cultural differences, prejudice, long distances, and disagreements about how we read the Bible or how we practice our faith have all caused splinters in the church. But Q&A 35 says, "The Son of God, through his Spirit and Word, gathers a community out of the entire human race." We have been gathered out of the entire human race for eternal life together.

I love visiting other churches and seeing how they worship God in their unique way. Even though I'm a stranger there, I belong too—because we're all part of the same worldwide church. Now that's one really big neighborhood!

What challenges to unity have you seen in the church? What can you do to promote unity in the church?

Visit a friend's church for a worship service. Talk together about the similarities and differences you see. How did it feel to be there?

Greed

Read Acts 5:1-11.

Let's imagine the church community again where everyone shared everything. Now imagine this. Your neighbor, a businessman, sells his business to raise money for the church. He comes to the church and gives a large amount of money, saying that he is giving all that he has earned to the community. But actually he's kept half the money for himself.

Why would he do that? How would you react? Could you trust this person again? The apostle Peter knew that Ananias was lying both to God and to his friends when he brought the money from his land to the church. Ananias fell to the ground and died. So did his wife, Sapphira.

This story is a painful reminder that even though Jesus has saved us, we are still broken people. We still make choices that put us at odds with God. It is in our human nature to be greedy and prideful. But Christ's way is to put ourselves aside for the sake of God's kingdom.

What's the big deal? Why did God respond so strongly? This is a hard story to understand. Jot down a few questions you have about it and talk them over with a pastor, parent, or mentor.

Have you ever lied to make yourself seem more holy or impressive in the eyes of others?

Your Gifts

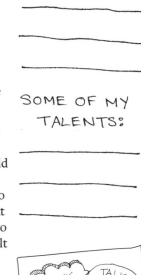

Read John 14:15-17a.

I have always loved riding my bike. I've been looking for opportunities to ride ever since the day my training wheels came off at the age of three—really, I've been riding that long! I'd bike to the beach, to school, to work, anywhere. Pretty soon, I was riding farther and farther, thirty or forty miles at a time. I started riding to neighboring cities just for the ride. When I moved to Kalamazoo, I made friends with some other cycling enthusiasts who were involved with an organization called ActiveWater. I told you before about the 200-mile bike ride we took to raise money for ActiveWater.

All eight of us who were riding on that trip had a passion for cycling. I believe that the Holy Spirit gave us that passion so we could use it for his kingdom. Sure, we could have just kept riding our bikes for our own personal enjoyment, but we wanted more than that. We wanted to help make a difference with the gifts God has given us. At the end of the day, we were able to raise enough money to put in a well in Zambia to help with the water crisis. It felt great to use my gifts for God's kingdom!

What are your spiritual gifts and special talents? What are some of your passions? Maybe you like biking, like me. Maybe you are a snowboarder or a musician, or you love animals or photography. Whatever it is, how can you find a way to share that gift with your community? How can you use that gift to show God's love?

SOME OF MY SPIRITUAL GIFTS:

_____

_____

_____

SOME OF MY TALENTS:

_____

_____

_____

THINK ABOUT IT   TALK ABOUT IT

Who do you know that is really using their gifts for God's kingdom?

ME AT AGE 3

CHALLENGE

List the top three ways you can use your gifts, talents, and passions to bless the community and glorify God:

 1.

 2.

 3.

Cornelius

How does the Spirit help us to be true children of God?

The Spirit leads us in the truth, breaks our stubborn habits, and makes us obedient to God (sanctification).

—Q&A 34

How do you experience God seeking you? How do you seek God?

Read Acts 10:1-8.

Though I graduated from Calvin College, I grew up in Holland, Michigan, which is home to Calvin's rival, Hope College. I have good friends who went to Hope, but I'm still a Calvin fan! Despite the rivalry, the schools are generally civil to one another. There is mutual respect and we even work together on certain projects. Still, when I wear my Calvin gear around Holland, I know some people look and think, "Oh, he's one of *them*."

During the time of the apostles, there was a more serious separation between the Jews (who were descendants of Abraham, Isaac, and Jacob) and the Gentiles (who weren't). Cornelius was a Gentile; but he was also a God-fearing man, generous with his money. An angel of the Lord spoke to Cornelius and told him to send for a man named Peter, who was a Jew.

Draw a sketch of this reality—God is seeking you, which causes you to seek him.

Cornelius was able to come to God because the Holy Spirit worked in his heart. As Q&A 34 says, the Spirit "leads us in the truth." That's what happened to Cornelius. Even though he wasn't part of God's chosen people, the Jews, the Spirit brought him to faith.

That's how we come to faith too. The Spirit works in our hearts to lead us to the truth. One of my family's favorite hymns says: "I sought the Lord and afterward I knew he moved my soul to seek him, seeking me." We seek out the Lord because the Spirit moves us to seek God. God made the first move. It's really cool that even though I thought I was seeking God, God was actually seeking me first.

Peter

How does Jesus' Spirit help the church?
The Spirit equips the church to carry out its mission: to make disciples from all nations and to tell everyone, by word and deed, the good news. This good news is that God in Jesus Christ forgives our sins and gives us new life now and forever.

—Q&A 36

Read Acts 10:9-23.

I've had some strange dreams, but I've never dreamed of a blanket full of animals I could eat. Peter must have been pretty hungry! But the Bible also says this dream was a vision from God. So what was God trying to teach Peter?

The Old Testament makes a big deal about things being either "clean" or "unclean." Jews like Peter were instructed in the Old Testament not to eat unclean animals. The strange part about this dream (other than, well, the whole thing) is that the Lord told Peter to kill and eat whichever animal he wanted. Even the unclean ones!

And just as God was giving this vision to Peter, some men sent by Cornelius (who we read about last time) came by and said that Cornelius wanted to hear from Peter about Jesus. A coincidence? Nope. God sent Peter the vision to tell him that nothing and no one is considered unclean by God. God's salvation through Jesus' death and resurrection is available to all people—not just Jews. Q&A 36 says, "The Spirit equips the church to carry out its mission: to make disciples from all nations and to tell everyone, by word and deed, the good news."

Peter had to see everyone as people loved by God before he could do the work of making disciples of all nations. We have to get over that hurdle too, so that the good news of the gospel will reach everyone in our world.

> **THINK ABOUT IT** **TALK ABOUT IT**
>
> Who looks down on whom in your school, church, and community?

CHALLENGE God says there is no such thing as "unclean," so we should treat everyone with the same love and respect. Try it this week!

True Faith

Read Acts 10:30-48.

Maybe you've experienced this: somebody says something like "Dude, don't move"—and they say it in a way that lets you know that if you move you might get hurt. Maybe a bee landed on your shoulder or you're about to step on some glass. Or someone says you need to go home right now, and you can tell it's urgent even though you don't know what it is.

When Cornelius had his vision about sending for a man named Peter in Joppa, he knew that Joppa was a Jewish community. He also knew that Jews didn't associate with Gentiles. This vision seemed to be asking Cornelius to do something strange, and he wasn't sure if Peter would come. It was a thirty-mile journey, more than a full day of travel, and Jews didn't usually come to stay with Gentiles. Yet Peter dropped everything to go and visit with Cornelius.

We trust our friends when they say "Don't move." And both Cornelius and Peter trusted in God that their visions were serious, urgent. Because of this, Cornelius and many people in Caesarea heard the good news of salvation through Jesus Christ. As Q&A 36 says, "This good news is that God in Jesus Christ forgives our sins and gives us new life now and forever."

There is urgency in this message of salvation. It's even more urgent than when our friends say "Don't move" in that serious tone. Do we take it that seriously?

THINK ABOUT IT   TALK ABOUT IT

Have you ever felt like God was trying to send you an important message telling you to do something?

DON'T

MOVE

CHALLENGE

Pray for three people you know who haven't received Christ as their Savior. Ask God to show you what to do to share his love with them.

One Church

REFORMED

METHODIST

What do you believe about the unity of the church?
The Holy Spirit builds one church, united in one Lord, one faith, one hope, and one baptism. This church includes believers of every time, place, race, and language.
—Q&A 37

THINK ABOUT IT · TALK ABOUT IT

It's hard to live what we believe—do you notice more unity or rivalry between churches?

Read Acts 11:19-30.

I've never been a huge football fan even though I was born in Denver and remember watching John Elway lead the Broncos to Super Bowl wins in 1997 and 1998. Lately, though, I have been watching more and more football—maybe because my roommate likes it so much. I don't have any allegiance to a specific football team. I just enjoy the action.

PRESBYTERIAN

Most people are committed to one team. Maybe you're an Ohio State fan or a Lions fan. You probably know other people who are fans of your rivals. Maybe your family loves one team, and your friends love another team. All these people (yes, even fans of your rival) have something in common—they like football.

BAPTIST

ONE CHURCH

As a church, we are one body no matter what denomination we belong to, what pastors we have, what building we meet in, or what kind of worship style we practice. We are one church with one faith, one hope, one baptism.

CHALLENGE

Ask around or check out your church or denominational website to find out how your church connects with other churches in your community and around the world. How do you partner together to serve God?

Some people say that the running game in football is most important but others think it's all about defense. Some teams have great passing, others are really good at special teams (kickoffs and punt returns—stuff like that.)

Like football teams, churches have different strengths. Some have talented musicians, others are good at hospitality or have great preaching. Even though we might emphasize different things, we all worship God. Q&A 37 says, "The Holy Spirit builds one church, united in one Lord." Did you catch that? We're all just one church. Your congregation—even your denomination—is just one piece in the wonderful patchwork of the people of God.

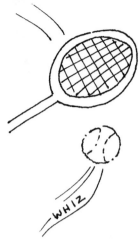

One Baptism

What do you believe about the unity of the church?
The Holy Spirit builds one church, united in one Lord, one faith, one hope, and one baptism. This church includes believers of every time, place, race, and language.

—Q&A 37

Read Ephesians 4:4-6.

Our high school tennis coach taught us to play a certain way. In tennis, some players are what we called "pushers." These are players who don't play aggressively; instead they try to be very consistent and wait for their opponent to make a mistake. Other players are more aggressive; they try to hit key shots in order to win the point.

If we are all part of one church, led by one Spirit, why do individual churches do things so differently?

My team didn't have any pushers. Perhaps that had something to do with our personalities, but it also reflected the way we were coached. Our coach expected us to be aggressive to win the point. But whether you're a pusher or a more aggressive player, you still have to follow the same rules of tennis. And all of us were aiming for the same thing: to win.

As a church, we have different traditions, different worship styles, different approaches to ministry, and different preaching techniques. We even differ on some things that are pretty important, like exactly what sacraments mean. I'm not saying that those differences don't matter—some of them matter a lot. But Q&A 37 reminds us that the Holy Spirit builds *one* church, and we share one baptism. Baptism, whether for infants or for older people, is a gaurantee of the cleansing we receive from Jesus' death and resurrection and of God's covenant promises extended to you and me.

CHALLENGE

Think these questions over yourself and then interview one or two other people from your church.

- What are some things your church is really good at?
- What "growth areas" do you see in your church?
- What do you value in your church?

Just as all tennis players play the same game, regardless of their style, all who worship the true God form one church together. Although our churches look different and feel different, we are all part of one covenant and one cleansing through Jesus Christ. God's covenant and Jesus' cleansing bind us together.

For Everyone

What do you believe about the unity of the church?
The Holy Spirit builds one church, united in one Lord, one faith, one hope, and one baptism. This church includes believers of every time, place, race, and language.
—Q&A 37

Read Acts 13:1-3.

I have a friend who has a passion for nature and wildlife. When we all went off to college he went to study environmental science. After college, he started working for the Department of Natural Resources in the Upper Peninsula of Michigan. He was able to use the gifts he was given and the information that he learned to fill the calling that God gave him.

We are all given different gifts and passions, and we are called to use those gifts for God. In Acts 13, Barnabas and Saul were called to be missionaries. They stayed in Antioch for a year, leading that church. When the time was right, they were sent out to spread the good news of Jesus Christ.

Some of us are called to be doctors or nurses; others, teachers or builders. (This is called *vocation*— not to be confused with *vacation*!) Whatever and wherever your vocation brings you, you are called to share the good news of Jesus Christ too.

We share the good news of Jesus with others both by acting like Jesus and by talking about Jesus. As the song says, "They'll know we are Christians by our love." Saint Francis of Assisi reportedly said, "Preach the gospel continuously. If necessary, use words."

Q&A 37 also says, "This church includes believers of every time, place, race, and language." Barnabas and Paul went out to share the gospel with all the nations and all people. As we read before, God's gift of his Son was not just for the Jews. It was for me, for you, and for people of every language, place, and race. How can you share the gospel with people you come in contact with?

THINK ABOUT IT / TALK ABOUT IT

What kind of work do you imagine yourself doing someday?

CHALLENGE

Ask a parent or another adult how they use their gifts and their vocation for God's glory. What did they say?

Decisions

Who is head of the church?

Jesus is head of the church. He guides and serves his church through its officers: ministers of the Word, evangelists, elders, and deacons.

—Q&A 38

Read Acts 15:5-21.

Growing up, my parents were the head of the household. Their decisions were final. I remember asking them when I was in high school if I could go on a camping trip with my friends for the weekend. They said they had to talk about it. I left the room and wished I could hear the conversation. I wanted to sit in and advocate for myself. I wanted to make sure they remembered all the good things I did and how responsible I was. I wanted to listen in on that meeting.

In Acts 15, we hear about a meeting a lot like this. But this meeting was about something way more serious than a camping trip with friends. This meeting was about what Gentiles had to do to become part of the church. Under Moses' law, Jews became part of the faith by a tradition called circumcision. It was part of God's covenant with his chosen people. The question at the council meeting was about whether or not Gentiles needed to participate in this sign of the old covenant in order to be Christian.

Can you remember any major decisions that were made in your church during your lifetime?

After much discussion, James spoke and summarized the decision of the group: they would not put extra rules on the Gentiles who were turning to God. James also did something else that was very important—he read a passage of Scripture that showed why they felt their decision was based on the Word of God.

How does Christ lead your church? Find out how your church leaders make decisions. Is it by vote? Do a certain number of elders and deacons need to be present? How much time do they spend discussing and praying?

I remember the anticipation while I waited to hear back from my parents about the camping trip. I wonder if the Gentiles felt the same way while they waited to hear about what they had to do to be part of the church. Q&A 38 says that Jesus is the head of the church, and he leads and serves his church through the officers. The officers are the leaders of our churches who meet together like the council in Acts 15 to spend time talking, praying, and studying Scripture. They do this so they can be led by Jesus to make important decisions about the life of the church and how we live together in community.

THAT'S MY FINAL ANSWER.

JESUS

Pastors

Who is head of the church?

Jesus is head of the church. He guides and serves his church through its officers: ministers of the Word, evangelists, elders, and deacons.

—Q&A 38

Read Acts 15:22-35.

I've only been a youth pastor for a short time, so I really appreciate having two wonderful senior pastors I can turn to for guidance and advice. But I've come to appreciate these pastors for other reasons too—they are great leaders.

Q&A 38 says that Jesus is head of the church and that he leads the church through its officers. The first one on the list is "ministers of the Word." These folks have a lot of responsibilities. They plan worship services and prepare sermons each week, leading the congregation in its study of God's Word. They administer the sacraments. That means that they supervise the serving of communion and they also baptize people. They do a lot of pastoral counseling too. If people have problems or need emotional support or guidance they often turn to their pastor. Sometimes pastors get called on to settle difficult situations like the one we read about in Acts 15.

I've had a chance to see firsthand all of the things my pastors do for me and for the church. In many ways they are just like all the other members of the congregation who are plumbers, accountants, homemakers, and professors. All are called by God to do their work. But pastors also have a special responsibility to lead the church as Christ's representatives. That's a big job, and I'm grateful not only to my current pastors, but to all the pastors I've had over the years.

THINK ABOUT IT — TALK ABOUT IT

What do you appreciate about your pastor?

CHALLENGE

Take a few minutes to pray for your pastor. Then write a note, text, or email of encouragement.

Care

WISE MIND

CARING HEART

LED BY THE LORD

Who is head of the church?
Jesus is head of the church. He guides and serves his church through its officers: ministers of the Word, evangelists, elders, and deacons.

—Q&A 38

I have different kinds of friends. Some are great at talking and listening. When I need advice or just someone to talk to, they are there for me. I also have friends who will do anything for me. If I need a meal or transportation they are more than willing to help out. When my car breaks down, they will come over and give me a hand fixing it.

The church has different kinds of leaders. Two very important types are deacons and elders. Growing up, I knew we had deacons and elders, but I didn't really know what they did. So what do they do?

When you look up *elder* in the dictionary, it will say something about someone who is given authority because of age and experience. That's true in the church too, although there is no specific age for elders—they could be fairly young but very wise. An elder in the church is someone who is considered to be spiritually mature, someone who can make decisions and provide pastoral care. Elders help their church members grow in faith.

Deacon means "servant." Deacons are servant-hearted people who collect money to be used for church ministry and for helping those in need. They may also coordinate a number of ministries that provide support to people in their church and the community. In many ways they are the hands and feet of the church.

I'm glad I have friends who play different roles in my life. Sometimes I need a friend who can talk to me. Other times I need friends who can help me out. Elders and deacons are different kinds of leaders, but both kinds care about people and are appointed by God (through the votes of the congregation) to serve in their roles.

THINK ABOUT IT   TALK ABOUT IT

What gifts do you think it would take to be an elder or a deacon? Can you see yourself in one of those roles one day?

CHALLENGE

Interview an elder or deacon this week. Ask what he or she does in that role and what he or she likes about being an elder or deacon.

Safety Line

Read John 8:1-11.

Maybe you've been on a high ropes course—the kind where you strap on a belt and harness, climb three stories into the air, and bravely traverse the distance between two poles across ropes. I remember doing one of these in middle school and thinking it would be really hard. I knew that the harness and safety line could hold me, but I didn't want to test them. I wanted to get across the course on my own.

I'm a pretty athletic person, but I'm not Spiderman. So I needed that harness and safety line in order to complete the ropes course. Even though I wanted to do it on my own, from time to time gravity got the best of me.

In John 8, the teachers and Pharisees brought out a woman who was caught in adultery. They reminded Jesus of the laws of Moses that said she should be stoned! They asked Jesus what they should do with her. The teachers and Pharisees were trying to trick Jesus into giving the wrong answer. The law of Moses said she should be stoned, but Roman law said that it was forbidden for Jews to carry out a death sentence. So there was no right answer to this question. If Jesus said "Stone her," he was going against the Romans. If he said "Don't stone her," he was going against the law of Moses.

Jesus replied, "Let any one of you who is without sin be the first to throw a stone at her." Faced with their own sin, the teachers and Pharisees walked away, one at a time. Then Jesus told the woman that he was not going to stone her either. "Go now," he said, "and leave your life of sin."

Before we get on a ropes course we may talk a big game. But sooner or later we'll need that harness and safety line. Knowing the safety line will hold me doesn't mean I jump off just to test it. And even though Jesus is our safety line, we don't sin deliberately just because we know we're covered. Jesus does not condemn the woman for her sin, but he tells her to stop sinning. He tells us the same thing. Jesus loves us and forgives us—and he tells us to leave our life of sin.

THINK ABOUT IT   TALK ABOUT IT

I wonder how the woman's life changed after that day.

CHALLENGE
Is there a sin in your life that you need to leave behind? Spend a few minutes talking to God about that.

What's the Difference?

What do you believe about "the forgiveness of sins"?
Because of Christ's sacrifice, God pardons me from all guilt and punishment for my sins and for my natural tendency to sin.

—*Q&A 39*

In Q&A 39 there is a distinction between "my sins" and "my natural tendency to sin". What's the difference? Why do we need to make a distinction between them?

Let's think back to the ropes course. When you are forty feet off the ground, gravity is a reality. Some people are fearless up there, but others are terrified of heights. I'm not one of them. I've made my mother plenty worried by my willingness to do stupid things high off the ground.

Some parts of the ropes course are harder than others, and at some point everyone has to rely on their safety harness. Gravity is a reality we live with, and so is our natural tendency to sin. Even though we don't try to sin, we are sinful by our nature. Just as gravity pulls us down, our human nature naturally pulls us toward sin.

Q&A 39 says that Jesus doesn't just forgive us for our actual sin—like when we lie about a homework assignment or about where we'll be on Friday night. He also forgives us for our natural tendency to sin. That means our salvation is more secure than a double-clipped safety harness!

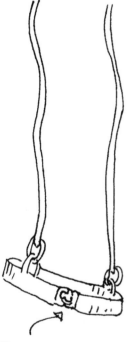

BUCKLE UP FOR SAFETY!

CHALLENGE

Sketch a picture of your 'natural tendency to sin'—how does that play out in your life?

Deceived

SERIOUSLY THOUGH... WHY IS IT SO HARD TO ADMIT THAT YOU MESSED UP?

Read 1 John 1:8-10.

When I was younger, I was pretty proud of how fast I could run. I thought I was the fastest person in the world! I grew up in church and always heard stories about Jesus' miracles and the amazing things he could do. One day I told my parents that I was faster than Jesus—after all, there are plenty of stories about Jesus walking around (even on water), but none about how fast he could run! I figured that I had him beat easily.

If Jesus and I were to race, I wonder if he would let me win just so I would feel good about myself. I do know now that I was probably deceiving myself by thinking I could run faster than Jesus. (I'm sure I named Jesus because I didn't know the names of any really fast runners besides me!)

The first chapter of 1 John talks about deceiving ourselves, but in this case it's about lying to ourselves about our sin. Sometimes we have a tendency to focus on a few things we do really well and forget about our natural tendency to sin. Or we think that the sin in our lives is really no big deal. It's great to celebrate the successes in our life, but we should never forget that we are born sinful and are made clean only through Jesus.

Worship services usually include a time of confession. Usually a prayer is read or a time given to confess your sins. It's followed by a Scripture reading that expresses God's love and forgiveness. God's grace always interrupts our confession with forgiveness, because God's grace is bigger than our sin!

THINK ABOUT IT / TALK ABOUT IT

If you were a parent, how would you respond if your child told you he was faster than Jesus?

I'M FASTER THAN JESUS!

I think my parents just waited until I was older, and then just teased me.

CHALLENGE

Be honest. Have you ever compared yourself with others and thought, "Well, at least I'm not doing THAT!" How would John 1:8-10 apply to that situation?

COUGH

Who We Were: Imperfect

DRAW ME ON THE MOWER...

AND

SOMETHING SIMILAR THAT YOU'VE DONE:

What comfort do you find in "the resurrection of the body" and "life everlasting"?
I trust that the new life I now experience will continue after death. By Christ's power my soul and body will be reunited and made perfect.

—Q&A 40

I did some pretty dumb things when I was younger. When I was in 4th or 5th grade, I couldn't wait to use the power mower to cut the grass. So I followed my dad out when he went to cut the grass and watched carefully. He showed me how to do it. Then he watched me do one stripe of the lawn and pointed out places I missed. For a couple of weeks he worked with me—each time letting me do a little more.

Finally came the wonderful moment when I got started and he actually went inside the house. I was outside cutting the grass with the power mower all by myself! Feeling the power of that engine under my control made me pretty happy.

I also had some good ideas for improving the process. After all, this thing practically ran by itself. I really didn't need to be walking behind it. I figured if I could stand on it while it ran I could save myself all that walking—and get a cool ride too! So I stood on the lawn mower facing backward with my arms stretched out to hold the handle.

What I forgot was that our family room has lots of windows. In no time my dad came running out, yelling at me. Looking back, I can see that it was a pretty dangerous stunt. If I had fallen, the blades could have cut my feet very badly.

CHALLENGE

'Life everlasting' starts now, but after the resurrection of our bodies we will be 'made perfect.' Try to imagine what that would be like. What will you be like then?

I still make mistakes but I continue to learn. I wonder if I'll look back on some of the things I do now and wonder how I could have been so dumb. But no matter how many mistakes I make, I know that I have life in Christ. Today's Q&A tells me that this new life will continue even after death. Then my body and soul will be reunited and perfect ... no more disobedience or dumb mistakes. That's *really* something to look forward to.

THINK ABOUT IT

TALK ABOUT IT

I wonder how often God watches us nervously like my dad watched me use the lawn mower.

Who We Are: People Who Belong

THINK ABOUT IT · TALK ABOUT IT

What is comforting about the promise of being resurrected? What would change if you didn't have this promise?

What comfort do you find in "the resurrection of the body" and "life everlasting"?
I trust that the new life I now experience will continue after death. By Christ's power my soul and body will be reunited and made perfect.

—Q&A 40

Read John 11:1-37 and 1 Thessalonians 4:13-18.

Around my house and my office I keep reminders of important things in my life—my high school and college diplomas, pictures of my family and friends. One of these important reminders is the picture and certificate from my baptism, and the devotional book my pastor gave me when I made profession of faith. These pieces of my past remind me of who I am—that I belong to Jesus.

It is interesting that Q&A 40 uses the word *comfort* again. Remember that word? We started this journey with Q&A 1: "What is your only comfort as a Christian? That I, body and soul, in life and death, belong to Jesus Christ."

This comfort is ours because we belong, and belonging comes with a promise—the resurrection of the body and life everlasting. Our souls and our bodies are going to be reunited and made perfect. That's a good reminder of who we are—people who belong to Jesus and who have new life that will continue even after death!

CHALLENGE

If you've been baptized, ask someone in your family to tell you all about it. Look for photos and other mementos of your faith journey. Or ask someone who is older than you what the promise of a resurrection means to them.

Diploma — Bryan Keeley

ME AND FRIENDS

Devotional

FAMILY ALBUM

Who We Will Be

Read John 11:38-44 and John 14:1-4.

When I was growing up I wanted to start making money. In middle school I began mowing all my neighbors' lawns, and pretty soon I earned enough money to buy a new bike and a guitar—and I had some spending money on the side. In 8th grade I started working every day after school as a school janitor. I worked full time in the summers because I liked the freedom of having my own money to spend.

I remember coming home with a paycheck, really excited about what I could spend it on. I talked to my parents and shared my great ideas with them. They gave me some advice: save it for college. That didn't sound like much fun. College seemed so far in the future that I didn't need to be thinking about it already, did I? But I took their advice and put some of it in savings.

When I was in college I realized something: I was broke! I wished I had saved more of my money from high school. But I couldn't change the past.

In John 14 Jesus tells us that he is going to his Father's house to prepare a place for us and that he will come back for us so that we can be with him for eternity. Lazarus was raised from the dead, and we will be raised from the dead to be with God forever!

When I was in middle school, I didn't plan much for college, but when I got there I wished I had. I wonder if we plan enough for eternity during our earthly life. What regrets will we have about the way we lived? Will we wish we'd been more generous? More gentle? More patient?

I wonder why it's so much easier to live for the moment than to think about eternity.

CHALLENGE

The best way we can prepare for eternal life is to live right now as Jesus told us to live, by loving God and loving others. How can you do that this week?

Drills and Scales

What good does it do you to learn all the teachings of this creed?
No good at all unless I truly believe in Jesus. Only by true faith in Christ do I become right with God and receive everlasting life.

—Q&A 41

Read Acts 9:1-19.

If you've ever been a part of a sports team, you know that practice makes perfect. You spend a lot of time perfecting technique, running drill after drill trying to get it just right. Then on game day you don't even have to think about it—you just enjoy playing the game. The same thing is true if you play a musical instrument. You practice scales so that when it is time for a performance you can play without thinking about it.

In the movie *Karate Kid*, Mr. Miyagi teaches Daniel household chores: "Wax on, wax off." "Paint the fence." Daniel wasn't sure why he had to do all these things until one day it clicked—he realized that in karate he could use the same motions as he used for these household chores. But if he studied these moves and never translated that into karate it wouldn't be worth much (except a clean house). The same thing is true of sports drills or musical scales. Unless we actually take that practice and turn it into a tennis match or a performance it doesn't do us much good.

Saul knew a lot about Jesus and he knew a lot about Christianity. He studied them in order to persecute Christians. He was like a person who does tennis drills but never gets in the game. When Jesus appeared to him in a great light on the road to Damascus, he finally got it.

What does it mean for you to be "in the game"?

All this study that we've been doing is just as important as practicing free throws or scales. But unless we get in the game, unless we have faith in Jesus, it does us no good at all. How about you? Are you still just practicing, or are you in the game?

LET'S PLAY IT AGAIN

CHALLENGE

Watch *Karate Kid*—the original version (it's a classic). Feel inspired.

MY FAITH JOURNEY

OTHER THINGS

Conversion!

Read Acts 9:19-22.

I am not like Saul. Saul grew up not knowing Jesus and had this remarkable experience on the road to Damascus that turned his whole life upside down. I've never had one of those experiences. But as I think about it, a number of people and a number of events were important in my faith development.

My parents have had a lot to do with my faith—they still do. There were also teachers who made a big difference for me, especially one, who I spent a lot of time talking to after school. He helped me see that working with teenswas something that I might like to do with my life. There were Sunday school teachers too who meant a lot to me. One went to my Little League games and watched me play baseball. He was my teacher for a couple of years in a row. There are also friends who encourage me in my faith and give me advice and guidance.

Working at a summer camp really helped me grow in faith and in my commitment to working with young people.

Sometimes when I read the story of Saul's conversion or hear wonderful stories of changed lives from people who really messed up their lives, I wish I had a big-change story to tell. But I don't. Lately I've started thinking more about the little stories, and I realize that they're just as impressive as the big ones. The way God worked in my life through a series of small things to bring me to him is just as amazing as if there had been a big ball of light that stopped me in my tracks. Because the results are still the same for Saul and for me—a relationship with the living God!

CHALLENGE

Make a timeline listing the important events in your faith. Leave some room for the rest of the events that will still be coming. . . .

BONUS CHALLENGE:

Ask your friends or family about important events in their faith journey.

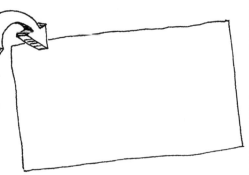

THINK ABOUT IT TALK ABOUT IT

What's your story? How has God been working in your life? What events and what people have helped bring you closer to God?

What's Really Important?

For it is by grace you have been saved, through faith—and this is not from yourselves, it is the gift of God—not by works, so that no one can boast.

—Ephesians 2:8-9

For a class assignment I had to make a PowerPoint presentation and give a speech. I don't remember what it was about—but I do remember being really proud of my PowerPoint presentation. It had cool pictures, great fonts, animation—even sound effects. This was a very cool PowerPoint.

When I got my grade back, I wasn't happy. I got a "D"! My teacher explained that the PowerPoint was good, but the content was not good. Then I realized that I'd spent so much time focusing on the flashy presentation that I missed the most important part—the actual content.

Sometimes I wonder if I have the same problem with my faith. I can get so caught up in thinking about what I could or should be doing for God, or what I've done wrong, or what I believe, that I miss what is really important: grace. The incredible truth that God's love is a gift, and nothing I can do will make God love me more or less. Maybe you're the same way.

Although the stuff that comes along with being a Christian (like living for Jesus, serving others, worship) is important, it's only the way we show gratitude for God's amazing grace. If I hadn't gotten caught up in the special effects of my PowerPoint, I would have focused on the content. In our lives, we don't want to get so caught up in the details that we miss what's really important: the incredible grace of God that is ours through faith in Jesus!

THINK ABOUT IT TALK ABOUT IT

Your life is full of tests and try-outs—do you ever find it hard to believe that you are saved by grace, not by how well you do?

NICE FONTS HUH?

WOW!

CHALLENGE

Think of a good definition of grace. Write it here.

GRACE:

Grace and Gratitude

Read Luke 7:36-50.

The show *Friends* (which was popular when I was in high school) follows a group of six friends on their daily adventures, romances, and relationships with each other. The nice thing about a show like this is that it isn't just about the people; it's about the relationships between them. Just like in *Friends*, today's story focuses on relationships between each person.

The woman in this story "lived a sinful life." She was desperate. The rest of the people in town looked down on her, especially the good Jews who followed the law every day—people like Simon, the Pharisee. When Simon gives Jesus a hard time about allowing this sinful woman to wash Jesus' feet, Jesus tells him a story about two people who owed money. The first person owed five hundred denarii and the second only fifty. (One denarii was a full day's pay, so even fifty was a lot of money—and five hundred was a whole lot of money!)

Jesus told the story to compare Simon to the woman (something Simon had already been doing). But Jesus didn't look down on the woman as Simon did. His relationship with her was built on grace. He loved her, and she loved him right back. The woman knew that she was sinful and that only Jesus could forgive her sins. She responded to Jesus' love by kissing and anointing his feet. She understood the magnitude of Jesus' grace and love.

Is your relationship with Jesus more like Simon's or like the woman who anointed Jesus' feet?

Simon, on the other hand, didn't understand the woman's expression of love because he didn't sense his own deep need for the forgiveness Jesus offers.

Some things in this story are different from today—for instance, we have different ideas about how to honor someone. So if someone came up to me and washed my feet I'd be a little freaked out. But one thing hasn't changed. When we realize how badly we've messed up and how much Jesus loves us anyway, God's grace becomes real in our lives.

Think of all the times God has forgiven you, cared for you, and shown unconditional love. Then spend a few minutes thanking Jesus for his grace.

Eh—What's the Big Deal?

Why do you say that you are right with God (*justified*) only by faith?
Because I cannot take credit before God for any of the good things I do, not even for my own faith. Only Christ's goodness and obedience can make me right with God. This becomes mine by God's grace through my faith.

—Q&A 42

Picture this: you're tied up 1-1 in a soccer game against your school's biggest rival; there's less than a minute of play left on the clock. Your teammate passes the ball with a great approach on the goal. You burn the one defender that's between you and the goal and rip a shot past the goalie. The stands explode in excitement. Casually you jog back to the bench—in a way that says, "Yeah, I know I'm awesome."

That's kind of how I picture the Pharisee Simon in the story we read this week. Simon has that "I'm cool" swagger—he's a Pharisee, he thinks he's got the whole God thing down. Maybe he needs a little forgiveness, but not nearly as much as that woman who is slobbering all over Jesus' feet.

While Simon is busy looking down on the woman, Jesus points out all the ways she has shown him more love than Simon. Simon didn't even offer him water to wash his own feet, yet this woman has not stopped kissing them since he entered the house.

Some of us grew up in a Christian home; we've gone to church our whole lives. Maybe you've learned about Jesus for as long as you can remember. That is a lot like me. I've read my Bible, prayed before meals, and done all that good stuff. Sometime I forget that nothing I do impresses God. I forget that it's only "Christ's goodness and obedience that can make me right with God."

But whether I'm the person who owes a giant debt or the one who owes a slightly smaller debt, I still owe more than I can pay. The woman who wept at Jesus feet knew that. Do you?

> THINK ABOUT IT / TALK ABOUT IT
>
> When have you felt deeply convicted of sin and seen your need for a Savior?

CHALLENGE

How can you respond to God's grace this week by showing great love to God? Make a plan and do it.

Life-Changing Love

Read Luke 7:44-50.

Recently my friend proposed to his girlfriend. He came up with an elaborate plan that involved a huge sign that said "Marry me?" and a deck overlooking a lake at sunset, a romantic dessert by candlelight, and fireworks. For my friend, this proposal was a life-changing response to the loving relationship the two of them have had for a few years.

In Luke's story of the woman who wept at Jesus' feet, we see the effect of the life-changing love of Jesus. His elaborate plan included an Easter sunrise after he died on the cross and rose again. His love paid the penalty for this woman's sin and ours. At the end of this story Jesus tells her, "Your sins are forgiven; your faith has saved you, go in peace." What a relief to feel the weight of sin lifted away.

That's what it's like for everyone who knows the love of Jesus. He changes us from the inside out, starting with our hearts. He makes us want to love him right back. People often cry tears of joy at weddings. I wonder if the woman's tears were tears of joy too. I wonder if she saw a new life, a new beginning ahead.

THINK ABOUT IT TALK ABOUT IT

How has Christ's love changed you?

CHALLENGE

Ask a Christian friend or family member to tell you how the love of Jesus has changed his or her heart or life.

Love

For God so loved the world that he gave his one and only Son, that whoever believes in him shall not perish but have eternal life.

—John 3:16

I grew up in a house with three sisters, one older, one twin, and one younger. I was trapped. I was sucked into watching chick flicks and lots of love stories. I figured that love was some soft emotion that made you feel good inside. At least that's what it was in the movies. But I've since learned that it's much more than that.

John 3:16 is one of those Bible verses many of us know by heart. We see it all over the place; someone is holding a sign that says "John 3:16" in the stands of a football game, or it's written on the faces of some football players. We see it on bumper stickers and billboards. Because we see it so often the verse can lose much of its meaning. "For God so loved the world that he gave his one and only Son. . . ."

Recently I watched *True Grit* (spoiler alert!). In this movie a character named Rooster Cogburn helps a 14-year-old girl named Mattie Ross avenge the death of her father. Throughout the movie Mattie annoys Rooster. It's pretty obvious that he doesn't like having a 14-year-old girl tagging along. Near the end of the movie, Mattie is bitten by a poisonous snake and Rooster picks her up and runs for help. He runs with her in his arms as far as he can possibly run, finally collapsing to the ground. With a small cabin in sight, Rooster grabs his gun and fires into the air to get help.

The love Rooster showed Mattie by running as fast and as far as he possibly could really hit me. This love required sacrifice. Now when I read John 3:16, I don't think about the feel-good love I saw on chick flicks. Instead I think of the sacrificial love that isn't comfortable but needed to be done anyway. "For God so loved the world that he gave his one and only Son."

WHAT IS YOUR FAVORITE MOVIE ABOUT LOVE? (IT DOESN'T HAVE TO BE A CHICK FLICK)

THINK ABOUT IT / TALK ABOUT IT

When we were growing up, my mom used to tell me and my siblings, "You have to love each other; you don't have to like each other." What's the difference?

CHALLENGE Think of three other examples of real love that you've seen in life, movies, or books.

John 3:16

REAL LOVE MEANS SACRIFICE

Christmas Story?

THINK ABOUT IT

TALK ABOUT IT

How does this passage help you understand the Christmas story?

Read Revelation 12.

Does your church do an annual Christmas pageant with the children and youth choirs? My church does. Parents marvel at how cute the kids are and how great the program was. My church is always looking for new ways to think about the Christmas story (although we have never used Revelation 12!).

The woman in Revelation 12 is sometimes understood to represent the virgin Mary, Israel, or the church as a whole. She is pregnant and about to give birth. There stands a dragon with seven heads ready to devour the child as soon as it's born. God snatches the child up to heaven with him and the woman flees to the wilderness. As you read about this, think of the child as Jesus and the dragon as Satan. You can see that this crazy story is the story of Jesus' birth, death, resurrection, and ascension—all in one shot! So this really is the Christmas story.

CHALLENGE

Share this version of the Christmas story with someone this week!

Imagine acting this story out for your next Christmas pageant. How do you think the parents would react? "Is that your son, in dragon head number 4?" That might make an interesting Christmas program. But it would also be a good one because the Christmas story is the first part of Christ's victory march!

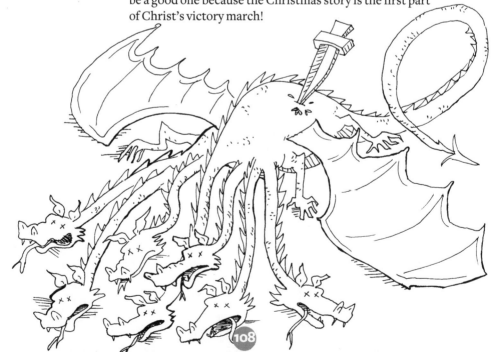

We Can Do It!

In 1942, the United States was in the middle of World War II. Everyone was asked to be part of the war effort, even those who were working at home. A popular poster at the time showed a woman known as Rosie the Riveter flexing her bicep with the words "We Can Do It" across the top. The poster was created to motivate Americans who weren't on the front lines. Our military needed the tools and vehicles we were producing; they couldn't win the war without the help of the people back home.

I thought about that when I read the passage in Revelation 12. In our everyday lives, we don't usually see seven-headed dragons. But we do experience the battle between good and evil. We know about temptation and we know about evil. Bad things happen.

THINK ABOUT IT   TALK ABOUT IT

What can you do to be part of the effort to overcome evil?

As I'm writing this there was a terrible earthquake and tsunami in Japan. I wonder if this is part of the war. The last verse of Revelation 12 tells of the war we are experiencing and encourages us to continue to keep God's commands and hold fast to our testimony about Jesus.

Just like Rosie the Riveter, we are an important part of the war effort against evil. But unlike Rosie, we already know the outcome of this war. Further into this story we read, "Then I looked, and there before me was the Lamb, standing on Mount Zion" (Revelation 14:1). Jesus (the Lamb) shows up, and he is victorious! We can do it because Jesus already did it. On the cross and in the resurrection, he won the victory. "Worthy is the Lamb, who was slain, to receive power and wealth and wisdom and strength and honor and glory and praise!" (Revelation 5:12).

CHALLENGE

Sketch Jesus, victorious and mighty, standing over the dead dragon.

"I Am the Resurrection"

JESUS HAS REALLY CHANGED MY LIFE.

OH LOOK... THERE HE IS!

POOF!

Read John 11:17-26, 39-44.

My friends sometimes tell stories that seem too good to be true, and they probably are. I always want proof. Legend has it that Hall of Fame baseball player Babe Ruth used to point to a spot in the stands where he was going to hit a homerun and then he'd actually do it. But I've never seen Babe Ruth hit a homer (probably because he died long before I was born).

The New York Times — BABE BLASTS THE BALL

In today's story Jesus shows up too late to cure Lazarus before he died. His sisters, Mary and Martha, are disappointed. Both tell Jesus that if he had been there Lazarus would not have died. Mary and Martha still refer to Jesus as the teacher and treat him with great respect, but the crowd who gathered speculated about why Jesus healed the blind man but didn't save Lazarus. The crowd knew Jesus was a great teacher, but they weren't as sure he was the Messiah. Could Jesus really conquer death?

THINK ABOUT IT TALK ABOUT IT

I wonder how Jesus' relationship with Mary, Martha, and Lazarus changed after this event.

Even when Jesus told Martha that Lazarus would live again, she thought Jesus was merely talking about the last day. Jesus meant much more than that. He said "I am the resurrection and the life." Then he brought Lazarus back from the dead, right there in front of his sisters and everyone else.

Sometimes I wonder why God doesn't prove to each of us, like he did for Mary and Martha, that he really is God. A nice miracle or two would do the trick for us, wouldn't it? Imagine how easy it would be if you were telling a friend about Jesus and he showed up and proved he was real.

CHALLENGE

Sketch a time you wish Jesus would show up beside you to prove himself or to work a miracle.

I trust that Babe Ruth's record is real because it can be confirmed by old newspaper reports of eyewitness accounts. Jesus' miraculous acts can be confirmed too. Not by the *Jerusalem Times*, but by the stories we read in Scripture. When you have doubts, read God's Word, talk to other Christians, and finally, look in your heart for the proof.

Jesus Is Risen

Read Matthew 28:1-10.

I recently watched the NBA Dunk Contest on TV. I knew I was going to see some pretty sweet dunks. Right away the contestants proved they were contenders by showing off their skills. I expected to be impressed, but that didn't stop me or anyone else from watching and reacting to what seemed like impossible moves. Applause shook the stadium as one athlete jumped over a car to dunk!

Mary Magdalene and the other Mary had heard the prophecies of Jesus' resurrection and knew that Jesus had raised Lazarus from the dead. They believed Jesus was the Messiah—but that didn't stop their amazed reaction when they saw the angel of the Lord sitting on the rolled-away stone. And it certainly didn't stop their reaction when they actually saw that Jesus had risen!

The angel instructed the Marys to go to Galilee and tell the disciples. There they would see Jesus. Filled with joy they hurried to find the disciples. But Jesus found them on their way. Astonished, they responded with worship.

THINK ABOUT IT TALK ABOUT IT

What is your response to Jesus' resurrection?

The athletes in the NBA Dunk Contest conquered the hoop, but Jesus conquered death. After each dunk the players hyped up the crowd and soaked up the cheers. But when Jesus saw Mary and Mary, he just said "Greetings"—not "Ta-da!" or "Did you see how cool that was?" Jesus conquered death—not just for himself or for a prize or title—he did it for me. He did it for you. Now that's really worth cheering about!

HE'S NOT HERE

HE HAS RISEN

CHALLENGE

Sing a praise song to honor the resurrected Jesus. Consider doing an Internet search for "In Christ Alone" and singing along with the music video.

Guards Deny

Read Matthew 28:11-15.

Conspiracy theories are not new. They have been going on for thousands of years. Do you know the conspiracy theory about UFOs and Area 51? Back in the summer of 1947 something crashed into a ranch near Roswell, New Mexico. The United States government said it was a surveillance balloon, but some people don't believe that. They think it was really a UFO with aliens from another planet. They think the government kept the crashed alien spacecraft and preserved the bodies of the aliens in a secret military base called Area 51. They claim that the government hushed it up to prevent the chaos it would inspire if the public feared an alien invasion.

Maybe it was a big conspiracy, and maybe it worked! Whatever happened, the Roswell incident hasn't changed my life or the lives of many other people—except maybe to add a little more excitement to the lives of UFO chasers.

What evidence do we have that Jesus was raised form the dead?

In Jesus' time there were people who denied that Jesus was really resurrected from the dead. A real government conspiracy did happen—the guards were actually paid to tell people that they fell asleep and the disciples came and stole Jesus' body. They spread the word and denied the truth of Jesus' resurrection. That conspiracy, however, didn't work. The disciples preached the good news of Jesus' resurrection and Jesus showed himself to enough people that the government just couldn't keep the news quiet.

Here's another difference: UFOs haven't changed my life, but Jesus Christ has. Jesus, who died on the cross for my sins and for yours also rose from the grave. He and beat sin and death once and for all! No amount of government cover-up can keep that good news quiet. Jesus is risen! He is risen indeed!

CHALLENGE

Ask someone you know to tell you what difference it makes in their lives that Jesus rose from the dead.